40 Presidents

FACTS and FUN

**Written by Joan Bumann
and John Patterson**

Illustrated by Doug Byrum

This book will tell you all about the presidents. Lots of fun puzzles and games are included, so get your pencil ready! You can find the answers to all the puzzles on pages 158-160.

Published by Willowisp Press, Inc.
401 E. Wilson Bridge Road, Worthington, Ohio 43085

Copyright ©1981 by Willowisp Press, Inc.

Printed in the United States of America

10 9 8 7 6 5

ISBN 0-87406-072-9

CONTENTS

1. George Washington............................ 5
2. John Adams................................ 10
3. Thomas Jefferson........................... 14
4. James Madison............................. 19
5. James Monroe.............................. 22
6. John Quincy Adams........................ 25
7. Andrew Jackson 29
8. Martin Van Buren.......................... 34
9. William Henry Harrison.................... 37
10. John Tyler 39
11. James K. Polk............................. 42
12. Zachary Taylor 45
13. Millard Fillmore 48
14. Franklin Pierce........................... 51
15. James Buchanan........................... 55
16. Abraham Lincoln.......................... 59
17. Andrew Johnson.......................... 64
18. Ulysses S. Grant.......................... 68
19. Rutherford B. Hayes 72
20. James A. Garfield......................... 75
21. Chester A. Arthur......................... 78
22 & 24. Grover Cleveland 81
23. Benjamin Harrison......................... 85
25. William McKinley.......................... 88
26. Theodore Roosevelt....................... 91
27. William Taft.............................. 96
28. Woodrow Wilson.......................... 99
29. Warren G. Harding....................... 103

30. Calvin Coolidge............................106
31. Herbert Hoover...........................110
32. Franklin D. Roosevelt....................114
33. Harry S. Truman.........................120
34. Dwight D. Eisenhower....................124
35. John F. Kennedy.........................128
36. Lyndon B. Johnson 134
37. Richard M. Nixon.........................138
38. Gerald Ford..............................144
39. Jimmy Carter.............................150
40. Ronald Reagan 154

GEORGE WASHINGTON
(1789-1797)

1

Born: February 22, 1732
Party: Federalist
Home state: Virginia
Term of office: 1789-1797
Died: December 14, 1799

"My movements to the chair of government will be
followed by feelings like those of a criminal
going to his execution."

When most people think of George Washington, they
think of a young boy who chopped down a cherry tree.
Some remember that Washington was the man with an
arm strong enough to throw a silver dollar across the
Potomac River. A few people laugh when they think of
his wooden false teeth. And almost everybody believes
he was the first president of our country. Only one of

these facts is true. Do you know which one?

Washington did have wooden teeth. He also had teeth made of whale bone and deer antlers. But he never chopped down a cherry tree in his life. And unless his pitching arm was better than any professional baseball player in the world, he couldn't have thrown anything across the Potomac River. The most startling fact? He wasn't even the first president.

The first president of our country was named John Hanlon. He was elected president of the Thirteen States in Confederation. That was the name the U.S. went by before the United States of America. After Hanlon, there were other presidents before Washington. They were: Elias Boudinot, Thomas Mifflin, Richard Henry Lee, Nathan Gorham, Arthur St. Clair and Cyrus Griffin.

George Washington was born on February 22, 1732, in Westmoreland County, Virginia. George never attended school past the sixth grade, but he was an expert at mathematics. He thought that his knowledge of math would make him a good pilot on a sailing ship. On a ship he could chart courses by using the stars and his math. At 14 he tried to run away to sea. But he was stopped by his brother and mother. He didn't give up his dream of adventure, though. George set out to explore and map uncharted lands in the new country.

By the time he was 17, George was so good at mapmaking that he was earning seven dollars a day. By age 21, he was a special messenger for the colony of Virginia. It was his job to deliver messages to the French army. At that time the colonies and France were almost at war.

Washington commanded a small group of Virginia troops in the first battle of the French and Indian War. George and his men came across a French scouting party. He and his men captured or killed all the Frenchmen. After that battle, Washington became the colonel in charge of all the Virginia troops.

George Washington was interested in good manners. He believed that a person should always control his emotions. As a child, he copied a list of one hundred rules for better manners. Some of the rules were "never pick your teeth at the table" and never stand too close to others when you are talking to them "for fear of bedewing them with spit." Washington followed these rules throughout his life.

He always seemed cool and in control of himself. But some people could see through George's mask. Gilbert Stuart, the artist who painted the famous pictures of Washington, saw through it. After finishing one picture of the President, Stuart said that if Washington had been born in the forest, he would have been the fiercest man among the savage tribes.

As a young man Washington was romantic. At parties he would dance with as many women as he could. He fell in love many times. He was rejected twice before he met the woman he finally married, Martha Custis. Martha was a wealthy widow with two children. The Father of our Country had no children of his own, but he loved Martha's children.

Although careful and exact in his career, he was very careless with his health. Washington suffered from small pox and malaria before he was 30.

While working as a surveyor, he nearly died twice.

Once he fell overboard from the small boat he used to chart rivers and almost drowned. Another time, an Indian shot at him from a distance of only 50 feet but missed.

Washington's fame and title as Father of our Country do not come from his presidency alone. Long before he became president of the U.S. he was working and fighting hard for this country. He was a delegate to the Continental Congress during the American Revolution. The delegates wanted Washington to become the Commander-in-Chief of the Continental Army. Washington was hesitant because he didn't want the money. He did allow the Continental Congress to pay his expenses.

The Revolution was a long and difficult struggle not only for America but for Washington personally. His army was a ragged group of farm-soldiers who wanted to go home every spring to plow their land. Washington tried hard to make up for their lack of interest. The winter at Valley Forge was only one of Washington's discouraging experiences. Many of his men died at Valley Forge of cold and hunger. But there were also people living comfortably who refused to pay their taxes for the support of the army. Washington's energy and desire for freedom kept the Continental Army fighting to their victory.

After the Revolution ended, Washington returned to his estate, Mount Vernon. He ran for the Virginia House three times before he was finally elected. During one of his campaigns, he insulted a man named Bob Payne. Payne jumped at Washington, knocking him down with a hickory stick. Later, Washington asked Payne to meet him at a local pub. A large crowd gathered expecting to see a fight. But when Payne arrived, Washington apologized and shook Payne's hand.

Washington was a member of the Virginia delegation to the Constitutional Convention. Because of his leadership as Commander of the Continental Army, Washington was chosen as presiding officer at the convention. A new government began to emerge after long months of debate. There were many fears and doubts among the citizens about the changes. The states were afraid to give up their power to a strong central government.

Finally, the Constitution was adopted. Everyone agreed that it could work only if George Washington became the first President. He was elected unanimously. John Adams was elected his Vice-President. The capital city was first New York and then Philadelphia.

Washington was a serious-minded President. He worked hard to organize the new federal government.

Washington was re-elected to a second term in 1793. He decided not to run for a third term. He died in 1799 and was buried at Mt. Vernon.

During Washington's term (1789-1797)
  -The first U.S. patent was issued.
  -The first U.S. census was taken.
  -Daniel Boone created the Wilderness Trail.

During 1789-1797:
  -"Bleeding" was the standard treatment for sick people.
  -The first successful balloon flight in the U.S. took place.
  -The New York Stock Exchange was founded.

JOHN ADAMS
(1797-1801)

2

Born: October 30, 1735
Party: Federalist
Home state: Massachusetts
Term of office: 1797-1801
Died: July 4, 1826

"I do not say when I became a politician,
for I never was one."

John Adams was 5'7" tall and weighed over 250
pounds. Because of his unusual shape, he was referred
to as "His Rotundity" or "His Roundness." Needless to
say, Adams hated these nicknames. Once, a newspaper
of the day printed a picture of the President with his
nickname printed across his rather large middle. Adams
threatened to challenge the next man who called him
"His Roundness" to a duel. Adams never saw his

nickname in print again.

As a boy, John Adams was athletic and slim. He loved any sport. He played to win whether it was marbles, boating, swimming, or wrestling. He loved hunting the best. He was so good at it that his father and uncles took young Adams along on their hunts. He seldom failed to bring back game.

The secret that John Adams always kept from his father was that he had learned many of his hunting skills from Indians. There was a family of Ponkapogas Indians nearby. Adams visited their lodge often. His parents told him not even to talk to Indians. But he found their way of life interesting enough to go against his parents' wishes.

John Adams loved books. He began reading at the age of four and started school at the age of six. He was always several grades ahead of others his age. His best subjects were math and spelling. He was the Massachusetts state spelling champion in 1745. He was only ten at the time.

After graduating from Harvard, he became a lawyer in Boston. His political career began with his appointment to a committee of the Continental Congress. He served as chairman for more than 25 of these committees. He was ambassador to France, Holland and Britain. He was also George Washington's vice-president for two terms.

Adams narrowly beat Thomas Jefferson in the presidential election of 1797. He was the first president to live in the White House. When the Adams family moved into the White House, it was still unfinished. The walls were so wet, seven cords of wood had to be burned to dry them. Adams' wife, Abigail, used the unfinished

East Room for hanging out laundry to dry.

The Adams family was a famous one. John's cousin, Sam Adams, was a famous patriot in the Revolution. John's wife, Abigail, was such a close advisor to the president that everyone called her "Mrs. President." They read and discussed everything together. She was one of the best educated women of the time. When the two were separated because of state business, they wrote long love letters to each other. Their oldest son, John Quincy Adams, was the only son of a president to become a president himself.

John Adams died on July 4, 1826, the fiftieth anniversary of the Declaration of Independence. Thomas Jefferson died the same day. John Quincy Adams was president when his father died.

John Adams lived longer than any other U.S. president— 91 years. His last words were, "Thomas Jefferson still survives. Independence forever!" Adams didn't know that Jefferson died that same day.

During Adams' presidency (1797-1801)
  -The Library of Congress was established.
  -There were five million people living in the U.S.
  -Washington, D.C., became the nation's capital.

During 1797-1801:
  -Growing long thumbnails became a new fad.
  -Johnny Appleseed became a folk legend.
  -Gentlemen wore powdered wigs and velvet knee breeches.

12

PRESIDENTIAL MONEY MATCH

Name the presidents who appear on these coins and bills. You may have to raid your piggy bank to answer this quiz!

penny   _____

nickel   _____

dime   _____

quarter   _____

$1 bill   _____

$2 bill   _____

$5 bill   _____

$20 bill   _____

THOMAS JEFFERSON
(1801-1809)

3

Born: April 13, 1743
Party: Democratic-Republican
Home state: Virginia
Term of Office: 1801-1809
Died: July 4, 1826

"Science is my passion; politics, my duty."

When Thomas Jefferson was ten years old, his father gave him a gun and told him to go into the woods and learn to hunt. The boy found no game even though he searched a long time. Finally he came across a wild turkey trapped in a pen. Tying it to a tree, he shot the bird, tossed it over his shoulder, and took it home. Jefferson was a person who always succeeded, no matter how he had to do it.

Jefferson was born on April 13, 1743, in Albemarle

County, Virginia. At the age of 17, he entered the College of William and Mary in Williamsburg. There he studied law. He also loved to play the violin. He practiced violin four hours a day along with the ten to twelve hours a day he spent studying.

By the time Jefferson was a man, he was 6'2" tall. He had very large hands and feet. His most striking feature was his bright red hair, tied in a pony tail. His hair and intelligence gave him the nickname "Red Fox."

Jefferson studied science all his life as a hobby. He enjoyed keeping records about the habits of insects and forest animals. Even as president, Jefferson rode his horse in the woods around Washington, D.C. He collected plants and studied animals.

He also enjoyed visiting and speaking with Indians. Unlike other white men of that time, Jefferson believed Indians were as smart as white men. He thought that he could learn from the Indians.

Jefferson was one of the best writers of his time. He wrote over twenty letters a day along with all his other memos and other governmental writings. At the age of 33, Jefferson wrote the Declaration of Independence. He used no books or notes when he wrote it. The Declaration was clear and to the point. He later helped write the Constitution and the Bill of Rights.

Jefferson was also an inventor. Some of his inventions are still used today. He invented the swivel chair, a revolving music stand, a letter-copying machine, and a pedometer, an instrument used to measure walking distance. Another invention of his, the dumbwaiter, is used in hotels and restaurants across the nation. Jefferson also helped to develop the American money system, the easiest money system in the world.

Thomas Jefferson had a long career in politics. He served in the Virginia legislature and in the Continental Congress. He was governor of Virginia, a U.S. congressman, minister to France, secretary of state, and vice-president. In 1800 he was elected president. Jefferson served two terms.

He brought a new spirit of democracy to the presidency. He believed in the common man. Jefferson was the first president to be inaugurated in Washington, D.C. During his presidency the size of the U.S. was doubled by the Louisiana Purchase.

Thomas Jefferson is also remembered for his architecture. During his term as minister to France, he traveled through southern France and northern Italy. In Italy, he became fascinated with Roman and Greek architecture. He drew detailed sketches of temples and pavilions, and he learned how the temples were built. When he returned to the United States, he used this knowledge to design the U.S. Capitol building. Many of Jefferson's buildings were domed like the Capitol.

Jefferson drew, designed and helped build his home called Monticello. It is the most beautiful and unusual of all the presidents' homes. Outside, Roman columns and arches blend with the wooded landscape. Inside, the home is full of Jefferson's inventions and gadgets.

At the age of 79 Jefferson went to work on a new project. He started a new college which became the University of Virginia. It was located in Charlottesville, near Monticello. Jefferson called Charlottesville the center of the wheel for all Virginia cities.

Jefferson planned the entire university. He designed

the buildings, decided which classes would be taught, and even wrote a system of rules for the students. He hated the way buildings and dormitories of the day were designed. He used his knowledge of Roman and Greek architecture again. Each building was modeled after a temple he had visited in Italy. The central building housed the library. Here Jefferson placed his best dome, the Rotunda. The inside of the dome served as a planetarium for students studying astronomy.

Jefferson personally surveyed the ground and supervised construction. When there was a shortage of labor, Jefferson provided on-the-job training for bricklayers. He even imported Italian sculptors to add classic art to the buildings. In 1825, the University of Virginia opened.

Of course, Jefferson was appointed the first president of the University. His office was always open to students. He would invite groups of students to dinner three times a week. He enjoyed telling them of the days of the Revolution and about his terms as president.

Jefferson had many unusual habits. He believed that washing his feet in cold water every morning would ward off colds. It must have worked, because Jefferson was never sick until he died. Jefferson hated to dress up. Once Jefferson greeted the British Ambassador in an old brown coat and bedroom slippers. Needless to say, the proper Englishman was offended. Thomas Jefferson loved food and even wrote his own cookbook. Jefferson enjoyed wine with every meal. After his eight years in the White House, his wine bill totaled almost $11,000. Jefferson kept a pet mockingbird, Bill, in his study. He taught Bill to talk, sit on his shoulder, and even peck food out of his mouth.

Jefferson and his wife, Martha, had six children. Mrs. Jefferson and four of the children died at young ages. Jefferson believed women should be educated. So he sent his two remaining daughters, Martha and Maria, to a French convent school while he was minister to France. Later his daughter Martha developed a love of politics. She named all her 13 children after famous Americans. One of her children was the first child to be born in the White House.

Although America flourished under Jefferson, he died penniless. Two years before he died, he was forced to sell his entire estate, including his personal library. Even with the sale of all his property, his grandson had to pay off $40,000 of Jefferson's bills.

Thomas Jefferson died July 4, 1826, the fiftieth anniversary of American independence. His last words were, "Is it the Fourth? Then I resign my spirit to God, to my daughters, to my country."

During Jefferson's presidency (1801-1809)
 - The Louisiana Purchase doubled the size of the U.S.
 - Alexander Hamilton was killed in a duel with Vice-President Aaron Burr.
 - The U.S. Navy sent ships to fight the Barbary pirates.

During 1801-1809:
 - The first successful steamboat was launched by Robert Fulton.
 - A professional prize fight was won for the first time by a black man.

JAMES MADISON
(1809-1817)

Born: March 16, 1751
Party: Democratic-Republican
Home state: Virginia
Term of office: 1809-1817
Died: June 28, 1836

"I would sooner be a constable than run for President."

James Madison was the smallest of all the U.S. presidents. He was only 5'4" tall and weighed under one hundred pounds. He was sickly and frail throughout his life. But he had a long career in politics. He is remembered as the Father of the Constitution.

Madison grew up at his family's plantation in Virginia. As a boy, he was not strong enough to play outdoors. His hobbies were reading and bird watching.

He always surprised others by getting more done than

anyone else. He started college at Princeton in 1769. There he completed a three-year program in law in only two years. Rushing through school was hard on his health. He had to miss his own graduation because of illness. Madison always pushed himself in school to make up for his lack of physical ability.

After college, Madison helped write the Virginia Constitution. He served in the state legislature and in Congress. He was an important delegate to the Constitutional Convention. Madison helped write the U.S. Constitution and the Bill of Rights. He also served as Jefferson's Secretary of State.

Madison and Jefferson were lifelong friends. Jefferson wanted Madison to succeed him as president. Many statesmen in Washington believed that Madison would do whatever Jefferson told him. Because of this and because of his size, Madison was given the nickname of "Jemmie." But Madison's brains made up for his lack of physical strength. He proved to be a strong president.

While Madison was president, the House of Representatives was reformed. Madison believed everyone should be represented in government.

In 1812 the House and the Senate voted to declare war on England. Outside of government, this was a very unpopular decision. The War of 1812 became known as "Madison's Ruinous War." It almost cost him re-election in 1814.

Madison was a bachelor until he was 43. The most colorful thing about James Madison was his new bride, Dolley. Aaron Burr introduced them at a Washington party. Madison fell in love with her immediately. She was pretty and active, and sometimes overshadowed

James Madison. The term First Lady was first used to describe Dolley Madison. She was so popular in Washington that a play was written and produced about her.

She was known for giving huge dinners at the White House. For the first time in Washington history, the White House became known as a social gathering place. Dolley always found unusual foods to serve at her banquets. Guests were delighted when she introduced ice cream to the White House menu.

Dolley was not only a good hostess. Many believe that she was a key advisor to Madison. At her parties she could always be found talking with senators and representatives about policies and politics.

Madison was also the first president to be shot at by enemy forces. When the British invaded Washington in 1812, Madison took command of a military garrison. He fired a cannon at the invaders. Later, when he saw that Washington would fall to the British, he fled east in his carriage with his wife Dolley.

Even though Madison was frail all his life, he lived to the age of 85, longer than most of the Founding Fathers. As he lay on his death bed, he looked up at his wife and said, "I always talk better lying down."

During Madison's presidency (1809-1817)
 -England and the U.S. fought the War of 1812.
 -Washington, D.C., was invaded by the British.
 -The House of Representatives was reformed.

During 1809-1817:
 -"The Star-Spangled Banner" was written.
 -There were 366 newspapers in the U.S.
 -The Loch Ness monster was first sighted.

JAMES MONROE
(1817-1825)

5

Born: April 28, 1758
Party: Democratic-Republican
Home state: Virginia
Term of office: 1817-1825
Died: July 4, 1831

"There is every reason to believe that our government will achieve the highest level of perfection."

During the Revolutionary War James Monroe was an aide to General Stirling. Stirling was known as a heavy drinker. And young Monroe made many of the drunken general's decisions. Monroe learned a lot by covering for the general. And he rose to the rank of lieutenant colonel in the Revolutionary Army.

After studying law under Thomas Jefferson, Monroe went on to become governor of Virginia, a U.S. Senator and Ambassador to France. Under Madison he served as Secretary of State and Secretary of War at the same time.

During Monroe's presidency many changes occurred in America. Florida was acquired from Spain. The Santa Fe Trail was opened. It gave an easier route to the Western territories. Five new states were admitted to the United States: Illinois, Alabama, Maine, Mississippi and Missouri. And the first public high school was also opened.

Monroe ran unopposed for his second term, the first time this had happened since George Washington was elected president in 1789 and 1793. He carried the Electoral College 231 to 1. This brought a new nickname to Monroe's years in the White House, "The Era of Good Feelings."

Monroe's personal life was run by his wife and two elegant daughters. His wife liked to be called "her majesty" by the servants in the White House. His two daughters were known as snobs. They always dressed in expensive party dresses from Paris. The three women of the White House planned parties without the President's knowledge. Because they were such free spenders of Monroe's money he died penniless.

Monroe died in New York City on July 4, 1831. He was over 6' and he looked a lot like George Washington.

During Monroe's presidency (1817-1825)
  -The Monroe Doctrine warned other countries that the Americas were not open to future colonization.
  -Five new states were admitted to the union.
  -The Santa Fe Trail was opened.

During 1817-1825:
  -The first steamship crossed the Atlantic.
  -The first machine that made paper was produced.
  -High schools began admitting girls.

WORD SCRAMBLE

ISONMAD   _ _ _ _ _ _ _

INGTONWASH   _ _ _ _ _ _ _ _ _ _

NHOJ SADAM   _ _ _ _ _ _ _ _ _

EORMON   _ _ _ _ _ _

FERSONFEJ   _ _ _ _ _ _ _ _ _

LEYDOL   _ _ _ _ _ _

AHTRAM   _ _ _ _ _ _

TM. NONVER   _ _. _ _ _ _ _ _ _

GAILABI   _ _ _ _ _ _ _

TSRIF YDAL   _ _ _ _ _ _ _ _ _

DENTIPRES   _ _ _ _ _ _ _ _ _

CELLOIMONT   _ _ _ _ _ _ _ _ _ _

TEWHI SEHOU   _ _ _ _ _ _ _ _ _ _

PENINDENCEDE   _ _ _ _ _ _ _ _ _ _ _ _

GALF   _ _ _ _

JOHN QUINCY ADAMS
(1825-1829)

6

Born: July 11, 1767
Party: Democratic-Republican
Home state: Massachusetts
Term of office: 1825-1829
Died: February 23, 1848

"I am a man of cold and forbidding manners."

John Quincy Adams' election and term as president began with a scandal. In the election of 1824 four candidates ran for president. Adams finished second behind Andrew Jackson. Since none of the four received the majority it was left to the House of Representatives to choose the next president. The vote in the House was tied until Speaker Henry Clay cast his vote for Adams. After his inauguration, Adams appointed Clay Secretary of State. Many people thought a "corrupt bargain" put

Adams in office. Because of this Adams was not elected to a second term.

As president, Adams refused to give interviews to newspaper men. Every morning at five the president went to the Potomac River to take a swim in the nude. On one of these mornings, he was surprised by a lady reporter. Anne Royall walked to the President's clothes lying on the bank and sat down on them. She refused to leave until he granted her an interview. It was his only interview during his term of office.

As president, Adams found it difficult to get anything accomplished. Adams recommended many federal projects while in office. He wanted more highways and bridges built across the nation. Adams also tried to push legislation through to create a weather service, to get more public buildings built, and to get a national university established. None of these things were done.

Andrew Jackson thought Adams had stolen the presidency. He worked very hard against Adams. In addition, Adams' "cold and forbidding" personality made him many enemies.

John Quincy Adams was born in Braintree, Massachusetts, on July 11, 1767. He was the only son of a president to become president himself. Adams married the daughter of an American diplomat in London. Their marriage lasted fifty years although they were not always happy. She once wrote a friend, "My husband seems to have no sympathy or tenderness for me."

In fact most of Adams' family life was unhappy. One of his three sons committed suicide at the age of 28. Adams read and wrote poetry as an outlet for his grief. In 1832 Adams published a 108-page book of his poems. He was the only President to publish poetry. He also kept a diary for over 50 years.

As a child he had many hobbies. He trapped and kept wild game, grew his own garden of vegetables and enjoyed swimming and horseback riding.

He saw many soldiers as a youth. He studied their actions and duties. The family home in Braintree was sometimes used as an emergency hospital during the Revolutionary War. The home was also used as a hiding place for people who fled the British troops in the North.

Adams was a fine student. He was taught by private tutors. His father sent for a French professor from Paris. He graduated second in his class at Harvard. Instead of attending law school, Adams clerked for a law firm in Braintree.

Adams was 5'7" tall and was almost as fat as his father. His eyes always bothered him and he was careless with his clothes. He even wore the same hat for ten years.

Adams served as a Congressman for 18 years after his term as president. He suffered a stroke at his desk in Washington and died a few days later on February 23, 1848. His last words were, "This is the last of earth, I am content."

During Adams' presidency (1825-1829)
   -The Erie Canal was completed.
   -The first U.S. passenger railroad was built. It
   used horse-drawn cars.

During 1825-1829:
- The Democratic party was formed.
- Swimming was first taught at the U.S. Swimming School in Boston.
- Webster's Dictionary was published.

NAME GAME

How many words can you make from this president's name?

MADISON

_____   _____

_____   _____

_____   _____

_____   _____

_____   _____

_____   _____

_____   _____

_____   _____

_____   _____

_____   _____

_____   _____

_____   _____

ANDREW JACKSON
(1829-1837)

7

Born: March 15, 1767
Party: Democratic-Republican
Home state: Tennessee
Term of office: 1829-1837
Died: June 8, 1845

"I only know two tunes.
One is 'Yankee Doodle,' the other ain't."

As a student Andrew Jackson was more interested in pulling pranks than in learning. He was the leader of a gang of school boys. They enjoyed turning over outhouses and playing poker. Jackson was often taken behind the school by his teacher, "Old Horn-rimmed," and beaten with a hickory stick.

At fourteen Jackson became a volunteer in the Revolutionary Army. After the war he lived in North

Carolina and studied law. He passed the bar exam and opened his own office. In court, he believed in short speeches and relied on his common sense. His grammar and pronunciation were not polished. But his speech made no difference to judges and juries. He could out-argue any "city lawyer."

His common sense in court brought him fame. He was appointed a Superior Court Justice in Tennessee. Jackson also served as a U.S. senator and a U.S. representative.

In the War of 1812 Andrew Jackson became a general. He commanded the American forces at the Battle of New Orleans. Later he commanded U.S. troops in Florida.

Jackson had common sense in politics and law, but not in his personal life. He liked gambling and horse racing. Jackson fell in love with a woman named Rachel Donelson. She was in the process of being divorced when the two met. They believed her divorce was final when they married. Later they learned her first husband delayed the divorce. This led to charges of immorality.

Jackson fought many duels to defend his wife's honor. He was wounded twice in duels. Because of the strain, Rachel suffered a nervous breakdown. She died shortly before Jackson entered the White House.

Jackson always enjoyed large parties. When he was inaugurated as president, he invited the entire country to a party at the White House. Over two thousand people showed up. When they left two days later, the White House was in shambles. Most of the furniture had been torn, broken, or stolen.

Jackson was truly the first president of the people.

His ideas were simple and easily understood by most Americans. He appointed many of his political friends to important posts. Jackson made one very unpopular decision. He vetoed a bill to renew the charter of the Bank of the United States. His vice-president, John C. Calhoun, resigned because of this veto. But he also paid off the national debt, and encouraged westward expansion. Two states were admitted to the Union during Jackson's terms in office—Arkansas and Michigan.

Jackson did not treat the Indians with good faith. He didn't honor the treaties the government had made. Thus he forced many Indians to give up their lands and move west.

Jackson had no children of his own, but the White House was always filled with them. His wife's brother had six children and they lived with Jackson. He acted as their father. President Jackson had a Christmas party for them. He sent invitations to one hundred families, asking the children to come "Frolic in the East Room." Jackson and Vice-President Van Buren played games with the children. When Van Buren lost a game of plate spinning, he was forced to run around the room, gobbling like a turkey.

The first attempt to assassinate a president was made during Jackson's term of office. An insane house painter who thought he was the King of England tried to kill Jackson. He fired two pistols at the President from six feet away, but both guns misfired. Jackson was unhurt.

Andrew Jackson was born March 15, 1767. His birthplace was in the frontier region known as Waxhaw, on the North and South Carolina border. Jackson was a slim, rough-cut man. He was over six feet tall and weighed 140 pounds. His nickname was Old Hickory.

Jackson died June 8, 1845 of tuberculosis. His final words were "I hope to meet each of you in heaven. Be good children, all of you, and strive to be ready when the change comes."

During Jackson's presidency (1829-1937)
- Most of the eastern Indian tribes were forced to move west of the Mississippi.
- Jackson became the first president to ride on a railroad train.
- Texas won its independence from Mexico.

During 1829-1837:
- The first American encyclopedia was published.
- Davy Crockett was killed in the Battle of the Alamo in Texas.
- The first individually wrapped bars of soap were sold.

WORD FIND

```
N T N E D I S E R P
O N O S I D A M E K
T Y Y A L E O P D R
G A E T S F L U F O
N N L L A W E P O Y
I K L J J L P B X W
H E O N A I D N I E
S E D J A C K S O N
A D A M S T S R I F
W H I T E H O U S E
```

Find these words hidden in the letters above.

President	Jackson	Yankee
Washington	White House	Madison
Adams	Dolley	Law
Red Fox	Yale	Indian
New York	Duel	First

MARTIN VAN BUREN
(1837-1841)

8

Born: December 5, 1782
Party: Democratic
Home state: New York
Term of office: 1837-1841
Died: July 24, 1862

"As to the Presidency, the two happiest days of my life were those of my entrance upon the office and my surrender of it."

Van Buren was so short that the first time he was called upon to speak in court, he had to stand on a chair. At the time he was 16 and an assistant lawyer. Many presidents sought a career in law, but none were as young as Van Buren. He began as an apprentice for a lawyer at the age of 14.

As a child in Kinderhook, New York, Van Buren had

many chances to view minor cases being settled in "court." At that time many cases were tried in the taverns by justices of the peace. Van Buren's family owned a tavern. He worked there throughout his childhood.

The Van Burens were of Dutch descent. They spoke Dutch rather than English. They referred to English as "Yankee talk."

Van Buren was the governor of New York and the vice-president under Andrew Jackson. He became president in 1837. He lost a second term because of the depression that occurred during those years. Four years later he ran as a candidate of the "Free Soil" party but only received 10% of the vote.

No president has had so many nicknames as Van Buren. To his friends he was the Little Magician, the Red Fox of Kinderhook, and Old Kinderhook. Later he picked up other nicknames like Little Van, and Petticoat Pet. Van Buren was named Petticoat Pet because he always dressed at the height of fashion. In the last years of his presidency his opponents named him Martin Van Ruin because they blamed the depression of 1837 on him.

Van Buren and his wife Hannah had four sons. His wife died when he was 36 and Van Buren never remarried. His political pursuits were always more important than his marriage. In his autobiography he didn't even mention his wife once.

Van Buren was 5'6" tall, slender, with blue eyes and long, curly red sideburns. He died of asthma on July 24, 1862.

During Van Buren's presidency (1837-1841)
  -A U.S. Navy expedition discovered the continent
   of Antarctica.
  -Van Buren established a ten-hour work day for
   federal employees.

During 1837-1841:
  -The first wagon train arrived in California.
  -The first woman horse thief published her
   confessions.
  -The first photograph of the moon was taken.

PRESIDENTIAL NICKNAMES

Washington .... Father of His Country
J. Adams........................... His Rotundity
Jefferson .... Red Fox
Madison................. Father of the Constitution
Monroe................... Last of the Cocked Hats
J. Q. Adams.................... Old Man Eloquent
Jackson................................ Old Hickory
Van Buren........................... Petticoat Pet

WILLIAM HENRY HARRISON
(1841)

9

Born: February 9, 1773
Party: Whig
Home state: Ohio
Term of office: 1841
Died: April 4, 1841

"Some folks are silly enough to have formed a plan to make a president of the U.S. out of this clod hopper."

William Henry Harrison was the son of a Virginia governor. He attended college in Virginia but dropped out to study medicine with a Philadelphia doctor. Then he gave that up to enlist in the U.S. Army.

At the age of 23 he eloped with Anna Symes, the daughter of a frontier judge. They had ten children during their marriage. One of their grandsons, Benjamin Harrison, became president.

Harrison spent most of his life in politics or the military. He was the governor of the Indiana Territory. He served in both the Senate and the House of Representatives.

In 1811 Harrison led the militia in defeating an Indian attack at Tippecanoe Creek, Indiana. He became a general in the War of 1812.

Harrison was elected president because he was a famous Indian fighter and general. Some historians think he was fair to the Indians when making treaties. Others believe that he was an expert at cheating Indians out of their land.

Harrison was 68 when he became president. He was the first president to die in office. His death was caused by pneumonia. He had the shortest term of office of any president: March 4, 1841 to April 4, 1841, only one month. He did not make any important decisions as president.

His nickname was Old Tippecanoe because of his victory at Tippecanoe. When campaigning for president with John Tyler, they used the slogan "Tippecanoe and Tyler, too."

JOHN TYLER
(1841-1845)

10

Born: March 29, 1790
Party: Whig
Home state: Virginia
Term of office: 1841-1845
Died: January 18, 1862

"The only people who seem to like me are my children."

John Tyler was an unpopular president. He was the first vice-president to take office because of the death of a president. His enemies called him His Accidency because of the way he assumed the office of the president.

Tyler was unpopular as a child, too. He hated anyone who tried to tell him what to do. He once led a classroom rebellion against one of his teachers. Tyler and the rest of the class tackled the teacher and tied him up on the floor. Tyler was expelled from school for the rest of that year.

After having so much trouble in grammar school, Tyler settled down. He went to Harvard and later received a law degree. He was elected to the Virginia House of Delegates at the age of 21. Later, he became a U.S. Senator and governor of Virginia.

Tyler's personal life was much happier than his political life. He was married to his first wife Letitia, for 29 years. They had seven children. Letitia Tyler died in the White House. Tyler remarried when he was 54. He married a 23-year-old beauty named Julia Gardiner. They had seven more children. The last one was born when Tyler was 70 years old!

President Tyler was a fine violinist. He loved French wine and poetry, too. He could always be found playing with some of his 14 children. It is said that Tyler was playing marbles with his sons when he learned that he was president.

As president, Tyler vetoed many bills sent to him by Congress. Senators and representatives called him Old Veto. Once, Tyler vetoed one of Henry Clay's bills. The bill was popular with most of the citizens. Angry mobs marched around the White House, throwing rocks and breaking windows. Tyler remained calm. He armed the White House staff and waited for the crowd to leave.

John Tyler was born in Virginia on March 29, 1790. He died on January 18, 1862. He was still unpopular at his death. The United States government took no official notice of his death. His dying words told that he knew he was disliked. On his death bed Tyler said, "Doctor, I am going. Perhaps, it is best for everyone."

40

During Tyler's presidency (1841-1845)
-Florida became a state.
-The House of Representatives made an unsuccessful attempt to impeach Tyler.
-Congress overrode a presidential veto for the first time.

During 1841-1845:
-Samuel Morse sent the first message by telegraph.
-The Barnum and Bailey Circus was started.
-Oberlin College granted the first college degree to a woman in the U.S.

PRESIDENTIAL TOP TEN

Put the first ten presidents in the order in which they served.

Madison _____

Jefferson _____

Monroe _____

Washington _____

W. H. Harrison _____

J. Q. Adams _____

Van Buren _____

J. Adams _____

Jackson _____

Tyler _____

JAMES K. POLK
(1845-1849)

11

Born: November 2, 1795
    in North Carolina
Party: Democratic
Represented: Tennessee
Term of office: 1845-1849
Died: June 15, 1849

"I prefer to supervise the
whole operation of government myself."

The inauguration of James K. Polk was unusual. The President and his wife, Sarah, did not believe in drinking or dancing. When President and Mrs. Polk arrived at the inauguration party, all music stopped and all the bottles of liquor were hidden. After the Polks' two-hour stay, the party continued.

The presidential couple's devotion to one another was undying. Sarah could always be found at her husband's side, serving as Polk's personal secretary. They worked together 12 to 14 hours a day. Even Polk's last words tell of his love for her, "Sarah, for all eternity, I love you."

As a boy, James Polk hated farm work. All children of the time were expected to do chores on the farm. But Polk thought farm animals were stupid and smelled rotten. Instead of doing chores he would hide in the barn and read or do arithmetic. His father apprenticed him with a clothmaker because James was such a bad farmhand. James didn't like that, either. So James was sent to college at the University of North Carolina in Chapel Hill.

Polk graduated first in his class. He became a lawyer and served in the Tennessee state legislature. A few years later he was elected as a U.S. representative and then was elected Speaker of the House. In 1839 Polk was elected governor of Tennessee.

When Polk ran for president, the issue was Texas. Both the United States and Mexico claimed the territory for their own. As a presidential candidate, Polk promised to make Texas a part of the U.S. He fulfilled his campaign promise. He also promised not to run for a second term. And he didn't.

At this time in American history new forms of communication were being used. The telegraph was first used in politics when Polk was nominated for president. The telegraph was used after that to carry news across the growing country. Also during Polk's term, an act was passed standardizing election day. Until then states could vote for the president anytime during the first week of November. Election day was made the first Tuesday in November.

Polk was 5'8" tall. He was skinny and his clothes always seemed too large for him. His nickname was Young Hickory because he was a close friend of Old Hickory, Andrew Jackson.

Polk was born November 2, 1795, in Mecklenburg County, North Carolina. He died just three months after leaving office, June 15, 1849, at his home in Nashville, Tennessee.

During Polk's presidency (1845-1849)
  -The U.S. and Mexico fought a war over Texas.
  -The U.S. Naval Academy was started.

During 1845-1849:
  -Astronomer Maria Mitchell discovered a comet.
  -Postage stamps were first used.
  -Gold was discovered in California.

TRIVIA BRAIN BUSTER

During which president's term . . .

1. Davy Crockett was killed in the Battle of the Alamo.

_____

2. The Loch Ness monster was first sighted.

_____

3. Gold was discovered in California.

_____

44

ZACHARY TAYLOR
(1849-1850)

12

Born: November 24, 1784
Party: Whig
Home state: Louisiana
Term of office: 1849-1850
Died: July 9, 1850

"The idea of my becoming president seems too
ridiculous to think about."

Zachary Taylor was born in Virginia. When he was
only a few months old, his family moved to the Kentucky
wilderness. He grew up surrounded by the danger of
Indian attack.

At 23 he began a career in the army. He became
famous as an Indian fighter. During the Mexican War he
became a hero. He and his men fought off an attack by
the army of Santa Anna, the hated leader of the

massacre at the Alamo.

Taylor was so busy fighting battles, he never stayed in one place long enough to become a registered voter. He didn't cast his first vote until he was 62.

His fame as a warrior took him to the White House. The leaders of the Whig party offered Zachary Taylor the nomination for president in a letter. Taylor didn't know he had been offered the nomination. He refused to pay the postage due on the letter. He got a second letter five days later. That time he accepted the letter and the nomination.

Taylor was the first president elected who had not served in any other office. He had not served in the U.S. or Continental Congress like previous presidents. But the American people liked his war record and his honesty. He did not come to office with friends to reward or enemies to punish.

Taylor was the first president to represent an area west of the Mississippi River. Taylor and his wife brought along part of their wilderness culture. She smoked a corncob pipe. He always wore baggy clothes and a tall hat pushed back on the top of his head. Taylor also loved to chew tobacco.

Taylor took his favorite horse with him to the White House. The horse's name was Whitey. General Taylor had ridden Whitey during the Mexican War. Whitey was allowed the run of the White House lawn. When Taylor died, the horse followed his master's body in his funeral procession.

Taylor was the second president to die in office. He became ill at the Fourth of July ceremonies dedicating the cornerstone of the Washington Monument. He had a fever when he returned to the White House. Then, against his doctor's orders, he ate a huge serving of ice milk and cherries. He developed violent cramps. Taylor died on July 9, 1850, after only 16 months in office.

During Taylor's presidency (1849-1850)
 -Two million people lived west of the Mississippi.
 -Taylor stood firm against southern states that threatened to withdraw from the U.S.

During 1849-1850:
 -The first woman doctor, Elizabeth Blackwell, opened her office.
 -New York State granted equal property rights to married women.
 -Nathaniel Hawthorne's *Scarlet Letter* was published.

QUICK QUIZ

1. Who was the president during the War of 1812?

   _____

2. Who was the only son of a president to also become president? _____

MILLARD FILLMORE
(1850-1853)

13

Born: January 7, 1800
Party: Whig
Home state: New York
Term of office: 1850-1853
Died: March 8, 1874

"May God save the country, for it is
obvious the people will not."

Millard Fillmore was born in a log cabin on January 7,
1800 in the Finger Lakes region of New York. His family
was poor. Millard had to go to work at the age of 14. He
was apprenticed to a cloth-maker. His years as an
apprentice were rough and unhappy. He and his employer
did not get along.

While he was an apprentice, Fillmore attended a one-
room schoolhouse. He fell in love with his pretty

teacher, Abigail Powers. She helped him to become a teacher, too. He then became a law clerk.

Fillmore opened his own law office in 1823 in Aurora, New York. Three years later Millard and Abigail were married. She was very devoted to her husband. She spent many hours helping him study law.

Fillmore's convincing manner in court drew the attention of the Whig Party. With their support, Fillmore was elected to Congress five times. He also served a term as New York State Comptroller. In 1848 his loyalty to the Whigs paid off. He was nominated as Zachary Taylor's vice-presidential candidate.

Fillmore became president when Taylor died in mid-1850. Taylor left many unsolved problems for Fillmore. The worst problem was slavery. As president, Fillmore signed a bill called the Compromise of 1850. This bill stopped slave trade in the District of Columbia. It also admitted California as a free state. These two parts pleased most congressmen. But another part of the bill was unpopular with the northern states. It was called the Fugitive Slave Act. It stated that a slave owner could claim any slave he thought was a runaway. Even though the Negro might have been free for years, the slave owner could take him back to the South as a slave. The Fugitive Slave Act cost Fillmore the support of the Northern States.

Fillmore received little fame for the good things he did as president. He sent Commodore Perry to Japan. This led to trade between the U.S. and Japan. Also, in 1851 when the Library of Congress caught fire, Fillmore and his Cabinet formed a bucket brigade to put out the fire.

President and Mrs. Fillmore improved the living conditions of the White House. When Fillmore took office, the White House had no books, not even a Bible. His wife, a former teacher, changed a room into a library. She was given $250.00 for the purchase of books. The Fillmores put in the first bathtub with running water. They also replaced the kitchen fireplace with a new cooking stove.

Fillmore was six feet tall. He was known for his handsome features and dignified manner.

Fillmore died on March 8, 1874 in Buffalo, New York.

During Fillmore's presidency (1850-1853)
  -The Fugitive Slave Act caused growing problems between the North and the South.
  -Northern abolitionists helped slaves escape through the underground railroad.

During 1850-1853:
  -*The New York Times* was started.
  -*Uncle Tom's Cabin* was written by Harriet Beecher Stowe.
  -Sixty-five million dollars' worth of gold was found in California.

FRANKLIN PIERCE
(1853-1857)

14

Born: November 23, 1804
Party: Democrat
Home state: New Hampshire
Term of office: 1853-1857
Died: October 8, 1869

"You have summoned me in my weakness. You must
sustain me with your strength."

Franklin Pierce was born November 23, 1804 in
Hillsboro, New Hampshire. As a boy, Franklin attended
the Hancock Academy. He later transferred to the
Francetown Academy. He was more interested in rough-
housing than studying.

At the age of 16, Pierce entered Bowdoin College in
Maine. He was still uninterested in learning. He found
out he was ranked the lowest of all the students. Then he

began working hard to learn. Pierce graduated third in his class. After college, he worked as a clerk in a law office.

Pierce began his political career quite young. He was 24 when he was elected to the New Hampshire legislature. Next he won a seat in the U.S. House of Representatives. He served there for two terms. In 1836 he was elected senator. He was only 32, the youngest senator at that time.

When the Mexican War broke out, Pierce joined the army. He rose quickly to the rank of brigadier general. During the battle of Churubusco, Pierce was wounded, but he continued to fight. He helped lead his men to victory at the battle.

Pierce wanted to retire from politics when he returned from the war. But in 1852, the Democrats asked him to run for president. The Democrats could not agree on any other candidate. Pierce agreed to run. Pierce won 27 of 31 states in his race against Winfield Scott, another Mexican War hero.

Pierce's presidency was marked with many firsts. Pierce was the first president who did not read his inaugural address. Instead, he memorized his speech. He was the first president to "affirm" rather than "swear" in taking the oath of office. Pierce was the only president who kept the same Cabinet through his whole term. He also had the only vice-president who took the oath of office in a foreign country. At the time, the Vice-President was in Cuba. And Pierce was the only president elected to office who was not nominated for a second term by his party.

He lost his second nomination because of "Bleeding

Kansas." A bill was introduced in the Senate to organize the new Kansas-Nebraska territory. The bill said that Kansas and Nebraska could become slave states if the settlers voted for it. Pierce backed the bill and helped get it through Congress. Soon pro- and anti-slavery supporters were fighting in the streets and fields of Kansas. The issue was not settled until Pierce left office.

The Democrats also disliked Pierce's ideas about Cuba. Pierce wanted to buy Cuba from Spain. The Democratic party supported this idea but not the next step in Pierce's plan. If the U.S. could not buy Cuba, Pierce wanted to fight Spain for it.

Pierce was troubled with personal problems, too. His only son was killed in a train wreck a short time before Pierce took office. His wife, Jane, was heartbroken at the loss of her son. She wouldn't go to her husband's inauguration ceremony. And she didn't attend any White House parties for the first two years of Pierce's term.

Pierce was 5'10" tall. He had black hair and gray eyes. Pierce was a colorful dresser known as "Handsome Frank."

During Pierce's presidency (1853-1857)
  -The U.S. paid Mexico $10 million for a strip of land in Arizona and New Mexico.
  -The Kansas-Nebraska Act was passed by Congress.

During 1853-1857:
-The Republican party was formed.
-The nine-inning baseball game was established.
-Railroad tracks were laid throughout the northern
  states.

MORSE CODE PUZZLE

Use the International Morse Code at the bottom of
the page to solve this puzzle.

— —. .   . — — — —   .— .   — — —. . .

.— —   .— .   . . .   —. .   — —. .   . —   — — — —   —.

.— — .   .— .   . . . —   —   . . . .   .

. . —.   .— .   — —   . . . .   .   . —.

— — —   . . —. .   — — —   . . — .   . — .

—. .—.   — — — .   . . .   — —. .—. .   — . — —

A . __	J . __ __ __	S . . .
B __ . . .	K __ . __	T __
C __ . __ .	L . __ . .	U . . __
D __ . .	M __ __	V . . . __
E .	N __ .	W . __ __
F . . __ .	O __ __ __	X __ . . __
G __ __ .	P . __ __ .	Y __ . __ __
H	Q __ __ . __	Z __ __ . .
I . .	R . __ .	

54

JAMES BUCHANAN
(1857-1861)

15

Born: April 23, 1791
Party: Democrat
Home state: Pennsylvania
Term of office: 1857-1861
Died: June 1, 1868

"At least I meant well for my country."

James Buchanan was born April 23, 1791 in a log cabin near Mercerburg, Pennsylvania. He was one of eleven children. Buchanan had an interesting and sometimes tragic life. He was expelled from Dickinson College for not treating his teachers with respect. But the college later allowed him to return. He graduated when he was only 18. He studied law for the next three years.

He volunteered for the Army during the War of 1812. He never rose above the rank of private. He was the only president not to rise above that rank.

When Buchanan was 28, his fiancee died. Some people thought she killed herself. After this tragedy, Buchanan vowed never to marry. He was the only president to remain a bachelor during his term of office.

After the War of 1812, Buchanan entered politics. He was elected to the Pennsylvania House of Representatives in 1814. He was elected as a member of the Federalist Party. In 1820 he was elected to Congress as a Federalist. But his friend, Andrew Jackson, convinced him to become a Democrat.

In 1831 Jackson made Buchanan ambassador to Russia. There he wrote the first trade treaty between the U.S. and Russia. Later Buchanan served as a U.S. senator. In 1845 Buchanan became President Polk's Secretary of State.

Buchanan tried to win the Democratic presidential nomination in 1852. But he lost the nomination. He went on to defeat John Fremont, one of the first Republicans, in the general election of 1856.

Buchanan's niece, Harriet Lane, served as his White House hostess. She became more popular than her uncle. Several songs of the time were dedicated to her. One song was called "Listen to the Mockingbird."

While Buchanan was president, several events occured that helped cause the Civil War. One event was the Dred Scott Decision. Dred Scott was a slave owned by a doctor in Missouri. Dred's master took him to Illinois, a free state. Dred sued his master for freedom. The case went to the U.S. Supreme Court. Some historians say that Buchanan "helped" the case. The Supreme Court said Scott had to remain a slave. Then the court ruled that it was illegal to outlaw slavery in the territories. The free states of the North became angry at the Supreme Court and Buchanan. The country was a step closer to war.

Next, a man named John Brown tried to start a revolution of the slaves. Brown led 18 armed men to Harpers Ferry, Virginia (now West Virginia). They captured the U.S. arsenal where guns and ammunition were stored.

Buchanan sent federal troops to capture Brown and his men. Brown was tried and hung. Again the anti-slavery forces were upset. The nation took another step toward bloodshed.

Finally, the election of 1860 took place. Buchanan did not run again. Abraham Lincoln campaigned on the slogan, "A house divided against itself cannot stand." He meant that the country could not survive with half free states and half slave states. The Southern states said that if Lincoln was elected, they would secede (break away) from the Union.

Lincoln was elected. A few weeks later South Carolina seceded from the Union. During Buchanan's last two months as president, six more states left the Union. Buchanan did not try to stop them. He did not want a civil war to start while he was president.

Buchanan retired to his home in Pennsylvania called Wheatland. He died June 1, 1868.

During Buchanan's presidency (1857-1861)
-The North and the South moved closer to Civil War.
-Seven states withdrew from the Union.

-Jefferson Davis became president of the Confederacy.

During 1857-1861:
-Gold was discovered in Colorado.
-The first transatlantic telegram was sent.
-The Pony Express was formed to deliver mail to
the West Coast.

PRESIDENTIAL NICKNAMES

W. Harrison............................... Tippecanoe
Tyler .... His Accidency
Polk............................... Young Hickory
Taylor...................... Old Rough and Ready
Fillmore...................... Fill 'em up Fillmore
Pierce........................... Handsome Frank
Buchanan...................... Bachelor President

ABRAHAM LINCOLN
(1861-1865)

16

Born: February 12, 1809
Party: Republican
Home state: Illinois
Term of office: 1861-1865
Died: April 15, 1865

"Government of the people, by the people,
for the people, shall not perish from the earth."

Abraham Lincoln was born February 12, 1809 in a log cabin in Kentucky. When Abe was eight, his family moved to a farm in Indiana. They arrived in the late fall and there was no time to build a cabin. That winter, they lived in a three-sided shelter. On the fourth side was a fire which burned day and night.

Abe's mother died the following year. His father went back to Kentucky for a visit. He returned to Indiana with his new wife and her three children. Lincoln's stepmother was a kind woman. She always encouraged Abe to better himself.

Lincoln attended school for only about a year. But he loved reading and learning. He borrowed books from neighbors since his family could not afford to buy them. Sometimes Abe walked several miles to borrow a book. Paper was scarce on the frontier. So Abe used a smooth board to do his arithmetic.

He started working as a laborer when he was 16. Lincoln earned 25 cents a day as a grocery store clerk, farmhand, ferryboat rower, and rail splitter. He was well-known in his community as a wrestler and storyteller.

When Lincoln was 21, his family moved to Illinois. Abe settled in a tiny frontier town called New Salem. There he worked as a storekeeper, postmaster, and surveyor. Lincoln decided to study law, but there were no law books in New Salem. So Abe walked to the next town, Springfield, to borrow law books.

At the age of 25 Lincoln was elected to the state legislature as a member of the Whig party. He was reelected in 1836 and received his license to practice law the same year.

Lincoln married Mary Todd in 1842. They lived at the Globe Tavern in Springfield until they bought their home. The Lincolns had four sons. Edward died at age four. Willie died in the White House when he was 12. Tad died a few years after his father's death. Robert, the eldest son, lived to be 82.

Lincoln was elected to one term in the House of Representatives. He returned to Springfield and worked as a lawyer. Sometimes Lincoln carried his legal papers inside his tall stovepipe hat. "Honest Abe" became one of the best-known lawyers in Illinois.

In 1856 Lincoln helped organize the new anti-slavery Republican party in Illinois. Two years later he ran against Stephen A. Douglas for a U.S. Senate seat. Lincoln and Douglas debated each other in several towns in Illinois. Lincoln thought slavery should not be allowed in the territories. Douglas thought each territory should decide the slavery issue. The Lincoln-Douglas debates received national attention. But Lincoln lost the election.

The Republican party chose Lincoln as their presidential candidate in 1860. Three other candidates ran for president, including Douglas. Lincoln stayed in Springfield during most of the campaign. He won the presidency with most of his support coming from the Northern states.

After his election Lincoln received a letter from a little girl in New York. She suggested the President-elect grow a beard. Lincoln took her advice. On his way to Washington, Lincoln invited the girl to visit his train and see his new beard.

He made speeches in many towns on the way to the nation's capital. In Baltimore, Lincoln was warned of an assassination plot. He left his special train and arrived in Washington early.

Seven Southern states had already left the Union when Lincoln was inaugurated. A month later the Confederates fired on Fort Sumter. The Civil War had begun.

President Lincoln believed that the Union must be

saved. He said, "A house divided against itself cannot stand." Slavery was the major issue that divided the North and South. In January 1863 Lincoln issued the Emancipation Proclamation. It said that the slaves in the Southern states were set free.

In November 1863 Lincoln made his most famous speech. He spoke at the dedication of a cemetery in Gettysburg, Pennsylvania. The Union had won an important battle there in July 1863. Lincoln's speech is called the Gettysburg Address.

President Lincoln put General Ulysses S. Grant in command of all the Northern troops early in 1864. Under Grant's command a Northern victory was only a matter of time.

Many young Northern soldiers sang a song during the Civil War: "We're coming, Father Abraham, one hundred thousand strong." The North won the Civil War because Lincoln refused to believe that they could lose.

The Republicans (calling themselves the National Union Party) renominated Lincoln in the summer of 1864. Their campaign slogan was "Don't swap horses while crossing the river." President Lincoln was re-elected by a huge majority.

In his second inaugural address Lincoln called for kind treatment of the South. He hoped for "a just and lasting peace among ourselves and with all nations." A month later General Robert E. Lee surrendered to General Grant at Appomattox Court House. The Civil War was finally over.

On April 14, 1865, President and Mrs. Lincoln attended a performance of a play called *Our American Cousin* at Ford's Theatre in Washington. A well-known actor named John Wilkes Booth shot the President in the back of the head. Lincoln was carried to a nearby house where he died the next morning.

Lincoln has a special place in presidential history. He was our tallest president at 6'4". He was the only president who had dreams foretelling the future. He was the first president to be assassinated. Because of his struggle to preserve the United States, Lincoln has become a symbol of democracy for all Americans.

During Lincoln's presidency (1861-1865)
-The Northern states and Southern states fought the Civil War.
-The first federal paper money was issued.
-West Virginia and Nevada became states.

During 1861-1865:
-Transcontinental telegraph lines were completed.
-The *Monitor* and the *Merrimac* fought the first battle between iron-clad ships.
-Oil was discovered in Pennsylvania.

ANDREW JOHNSON
(1865-1869)

17

Born: December 29, 1808
  in North Carolina
Party: Union (Republican)
Home state: Tennessee
Term of office: 1865-1869
Died: July 31, 1875

"Duties have been mine; consequences are God's."

Andrew Johnson was born in Raleigh, North Carolina on December 29, 1808. His family was so poor that he could not go to school. When he was 13 he was apprenticed to a tailor. He learned to read but he did not know how to write.

Johnson hated being an apprentice. When he was 16 he ran away to South Carolina. Then he moved to Greeneville, Tennessee to open his own tailoring business. He married Eliza McCardle, a young school teacher.

While Andrew sewed clothes, Eliza taught him how to write and do arithmetic.

In Greeneville he became very interested in politics. He was elected mayor when he was only 21. Andrew wanted very much to be a representative to the state legislature. But during this time, land owners were the only people who became representatives. Johnson fought a hard battle and was elected. He then moved to the Congress. Next he served as governor of Tennessee and then in the U.S. Senate.

When Lincoln was elected to a second term in 1864, Johnson was elected as his vice-president. The Republican party used the name Union party that year. Johnson was vice-president for only a few weeks. Lincoln was assassinated, and Johnson became president.

Johnson tried to carry out the policies that Lincoln had started. But the radical Republicans were in control of Congress. They disagreed with Johnson's policies. President Johnson used his veto power to fight Congress. To get even, the Congress overrode his vetoes. Congress also passed the Tenure of Office Act. This law said the President could not fire the members of his own Cabinet. Johnson claimed this law was unconstitutional.

In 1868 this new law led to a showdown between the President and Congress. The House of Representatives voted to impeach Johnson. Impeachment is the first step in removing a president from office.

Next Johnson was tried by the Senate. The trial lasted more than two months. The Senators voted three times. Each time the vote was one short of the two-thirds majority needed to convict Johnson and remove him from office.

Johnson did not run for another term. Later, he returned to Congress as a senator from Tennessee.

Johnson was a stocky 5'10". He had unruly hair, a grim mouth and heavy brows. He was the only president who made most of his own clothes. When he was governor of Tennessee he even made a suit of clothes for the governor of Kentucky.

Andrew Johnson died of a stroke on July 31, 1875 at Carter Station, Tennessee.

During Johnson's presidency (1865-1869)
  -Alaska was purchased from Russia for two cents an acre.
  -Johnson became the only president impeached by the House of Representatives.
  -The Reconstruction era brought many changes to the South.

During 1865-1869:
  -The first nickels were issued.
  -The first big cattle drive took place. Cowboys drove 260,000 head from Texas to Kansas.
  -The typewriter was patented.

PRESIDENTIAL QUIZ

1. He sewed his own clothes.

   _____

2. He had dreams foretelling the future.

   _____

3. He was called Petticoat Pet.

   _____

4. He didn't like working on his father's farm.

   _____

5. He weighed less than 100 pounds.

   _____

6. He fought in a famous Indian battle at Tippecanoe
   Creek. _____

7. He had wooden teeth.

   _____

8. He was expelled from school for tying up a teacher.

   _____

9. He put a bathtub and cooking stove in the White
   House._____

10. He was called Handsome Frank.

    _____

11. He wrote poetry.

    _____

ULYSSES S. GRANT
(1869-1877)

18

Born: April 27, 1822
Party: Republican
Home state: Illinois
Term of office: 1869-1877
Died: July, 23, 1885

"The art of war is simple. Find out where the enemy is. Get at him as soon as you can. Strike at him as hard as you can and keep moving."

Ulysses S. Grant's parents named him Hiram Ulysses Grant when he was born. But he didn't like his initials (H.U.G.). When Ulysses entered West Point, his name was recorded as Ulysses Simpson Grant. Simpson was his mother's maiden name. He decided that he liked the name U.S. Grant better.

Grant graduated from West Point near the bottom of

his class. He served in the Mexican War and rose to the rank of captain. But when the Army sent Grant to California, he missed his family and started drinking. Because of this, he left the Army.

Grant returned home after his resignation. He tried farming, but drought wiped out his farm. Grant worked for a while selling real estate but could not make any sales. He went to work in a store owned by his father. At 38 Grant seemed washed up. But the Civil War began and Grant rejoined the Army.

Because of a lack of trained soldiers, Grant was asked to command a regiment of volunteers from Illinois. His regiment became one of the best in the Western Army. His leadership was noticed by President Lincoln. Grant rose to the rank of brigadier general.

Grant won his first Civil War battles at Fort Henry and Fort Donnelson. At Fort Donnelson, he demanded the complete surrender of the fort. From then on, Grant was known as "Unconditional Surrender" Grant. A few months later, he won the bloody Battle of Shiloh.

After Shiloh, rumors started that Grant was drinking again. Because of this, Grant was not promoted. However, none of the other generals proved as successful as Grant. And he was soon promoted to major general.

With Grant in command, the Western Union Army captured first Vicksburg, Mississippi and then Chattanooga, Tennessee. These two victories cut the Confederacy in half. In the spring of 1864, Grant was promoted to general of all the Union Armies.

From that moment on, the Union Armies attacked the Confederate Armies like bulldogs, never letting them rest. The Civil War became a grinding, brutal attack by the North. Finally, the Confederate Armies could fight no more. On April 9, 1865, General Robert E. Lee surrendered to General Grant at Appomattox Court House. Almost a half million men died in the Civil War.

Grant was a national hero. The Republicans saw this. They nominated Grant as their presidential candidate. Grant easily won the election.

President Grant loved the American wilderness. He wanted future generations of Americans to see the natural beauty of their country. As president, he had large areas of wilderness set aside for parks. Our most famous national park, Yellowstone, was established while Grant was president.

Grant and his wife, Julia, remodeled the White House. They enjoyed entertaining guests from all over the world. Although Grant served alcohol in the White House, he did not drink. But Grant did smoke at least 20 cigars a day.

The Republicans nominated Grant for a second term in the White House. He had an easy time being re-elected.

Grant's second term was marked by corruption in government and business. Many government officials made illegal deals. Dishonest Northern politicians invaded the South. They were called Carpetbaggers. They took bribes and were dishonest in their dealings with Southern leaders. And they used the South's defeat to make themselves rich. Grant took no action to clean up dishonesty in business and government.

After leaving the White House, the Grants took a long trip to Europe. When they returned, Grant invested all their savings in a banking company. He lost all his money when the company failed.

Grant learned that he was dying of throat cancer. He wrote his autobiography so that his family would not be penniless. Mark Twain helped get the book published. It was a success and brought the Grant family over half a million dollars.

Ulysses S. Grant died in New York on July 23, 1885.

During Grant's presidency (1869-1877)
-Two members of Congress and five federal judges resigned to avoid impeachment.
-General Custer and his men were killed by Indians at the Battle of the Little Big Horn.
-The U.S. celebrated its 100th birthday.

During 1869-1877:
-Mark Twain wrote *The Adventures of Tom Sawyer.*
-The first college football game was played in 1869 between Princeton and Rutgers.
-Alexander Graham Bell patented the telephone.

RUTHERFORD B. HAYES
(1877-1881)

19

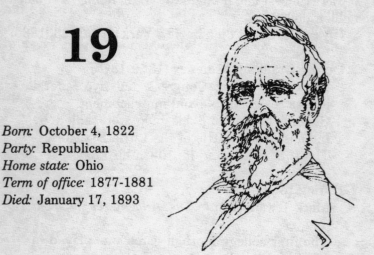

Born: October 4, 1822
Party: Republican
Home state: Ohio
Term of office: 1877-1881
Died: January 17, 1893

"No one ever left the presidency with less regret."

Rutherford B. Hayes was born October 4, 1822 in Delaware, Ohio. He went to a private school in New England, Kenyon College in Ohio, and Harvard Law School. He graduated from Harvard at the top of his class. Hayes opened a law practice in Ohio after graduation. He won fame as a defense lawyer for fugitive slaves.

Hayes volunteered for service when the Civil War began. He was a major in the Ohio 23rd Infantry. Hayes fought in many battles. He was wounded four times and had four horses shot out from under him. He was a hero at the bloody Battle of South Mountain. Hayes rose to the rank of general.

Hayes was still fighting in the Civil War when Ohio Republicans nominated him for Congress. He did not campaign. He said his job as a soldier was unfinished. But the people of Ohio elected him to the House of Representatives.

His record as a congressman pleased Ohioans. They liked his ideas and his honesty. The people of Ohio elected Hayes governor of their state in 1867. He was the first governor in Ohio's history to win three terms.

Hayes soon became popular with Republicans across the country. They thought he was a strong leader who would make a good president. In 1876 they nominated him to run for president. He ran against Democrat Samuel Tilden in the election.

The campaign issue of 1876 was corruption in government. After the Civil War the South was occupied by federal troops. Many Southern politicians were dishonest. The Republicans thought Hayes would stop corruption in the South. After all, he had been an honest and strong governor. But in his bid for the presidency, Hayes was stained by corruption himself.

On election day, Tilden received 250,000 more popular votes than Hayes. But the Republicans said that blacks had been kept from voting in Louisiana, South Carolina, and Florida. The election was turned over to a special committee. The Democrats and Republicans made a deal. Hayes would be president if he would agree to withdraw the troops from the South. Only 56 hours

73

before the inauguration, the House approved Hayes as the next president.

Hayes' shady election was not his only problem. His presidency was marred by violent labor strikes and riots. Congress was controlled by Democrats who would not support the President's ideas.

President Hayes and his wife, Lucy, were very religious. They did not serve alcoholic drinks at the White House. Because of this the First Lady was called Lemonade Lucy.

Hayes did not run for a second term as president. He died in Ohio in 1893.

During Hayes' presidency (1877-1881)
  -Federal troops were withdrawn from the South.
  -The government issued the first silver dollars.
  -Railroad workers staged the first national strike.

During 1877-1881:
  -The first bicycle was sold.
  -Frank Woolworth opened the first five-and-ten-cent store.
  -Edison patented the phonograph.

JAMES A. GARFIELD
(1881)

20

Born: November 19, 1831
Party: Republican
Home state: Ohio
Term of office: 1881
Died: September 19,1881

"What is there in this place that a man should
ever want to get into it?"

James A. Garfield was born November 19, 1831 in
Orange, Ohio. He was the last president born in a log
cabin. His father died when James was only a year and a
half old. His mother kept the family farm going, but they
were very poor.

Garfield started school at the age of three. As a boy he
loved reading and wanted to go to college. He worked
hard at odd jobs to earn money for school.

Garfield attended Hiram College in Ohio. He tutored other students in Greek and Latin. One of his students was his future wife, Lucretia Rudolph.

After graduating from Williams College in Massachusetts, Garfield returned to Hiram College as a professor of Greek and Latin. At the age of 26 he became president of the college. He married Lucretia the next year. They had seven children. Lucretia taught all their children Latin.

In addition to his work as college president, Garfield studied law and was a lay minister. He was elected to the state senate in 1859.

Garfield was an officer in the Civil War. He served in the battles of Shiloh, Corinth, and Chickamauga. At the age of 30, Garfield became one of the youngest generals in the Union Army.

Next, he was elected to Congress and served for the next 17 years. In 1880 the Republicans could not agree on their presidential candidate. Finally they chose James A. Garfield. He was elected by a slim margin.

Garfield was the second president to be killed while in office. On July 2, 1881, Charles Guiteau shot the President in a railway station in Washington, D.C. Guiteau was angry because he had not been appointed to the U.S. Embassy in Paris.

President Garfield died two months later. His only official act as president was to sign the paper ordering Guiteau hung.

Garfield was six feet tall with blond hair and blue eyes. He had broad shoulders and an athletic build.

During Garfield's presidency (1881)
- Peddlars in the Capitol building sold stoves, buggy whips, snake oil, mousetraps, kitchen utensils, and pianos.
- Alexander Graham Bell was called to the White House to help locate the bullet still lodged in President Garfield.
- Concerned citizens sent many different medicines to the White House for the injured President.

During 1881:
- The American Red Cross was founded.
- The first U.S. tennis championship was held.
- Horatio Alger's stories for boys were very popular. The stories told about poor boys who worked hard and did well in life.

TRUE OR FALSE

1. Andrew Jackson's nickname was Old Hickory. _____
2. George Washington chopped down a cherry tree when he was a boy. _____
3. Abraham Lincoln sometimes carried his papers inside his tall stovepipe hat. _____

CHESTER A. ARTHUR
(1881-1885)

21

Born: October 5, 1829
Party: Republican
Home state: New York
Term of office: 1881-1885
Died: November 18, 1886

"Heaven save us."

Chester Alan Arthur was born in Fairfield, Vermont. He always gave his birthdate as October 5, 1830. That is the date given in many history books. But a century after Chester's birth, the Arthur family Bible was given to the New York Public Library. Historians learned Arthur was really born in 1829.

His political opponents claimed Arthur was actually born in Canada. If that were true, he would not have been eligible for the presidency. Today some historians agree that Arthur was not born in the U.S.

Chester's nickname as a boy was Chet. His father was a Baptist preacher in New York State.

Chet entered Union College at the age of 15. He belonged to a social fraternity and an honor fraternity, Phi Beta Kappa. Only six members of his class were chosen for this honor. Arthur graduated from college when he was 18. Next he became a teacher and attended law school.

In 1853 he joined a law firm in New York City. As a lawyer he was sympathetic to civil rights cases of that time. His strong anti-slavery feelings earned him a lot of publicity. In one case he helped six slaves win their freedom. He also helped a black woman named Lizzie Jennings. She was thrown off a trolley car because she was black. Arthur helped her sue the trolley company. They won $500 in damages.

Arthur was 29 when he married Ellen Herndon. She was a talented singer. They had three children. After twenty years of marriage, Ellen died of pneumonia. She did not live long enough to see her husband become president. Arthur was heartbroken by her death.

During the Civil War Arthur served as quartermaster general for New York State. He used the title "general" for the rest of his life.

Arthur was active in the Republican Party. He was appointed to several political jobs. He was fired from one job by President Hayes.

Chester Arthur became vice-president in 1881. At that time the Democrats and Republicans were evenly divided in the Senate. Arthur had to cast many tie-breaking votes as presiding officer of the Senate. When

Garfield died, Arthur became president.

President Arthur turned his back on the political bosses of the time. He succeeded in running an honest government. This earned him the nickname of Gentleman Boss.

During his presidency Arthur urged Congress to change the way U.S. government employees were hired. He had many good ideas to improve government. But the Democratic majority in Congress did not support Arthur's ideas.

He remodeled the White House and added an elevator. Twenty-four wagonloads of furniture were sold and replaced with furniture the President liked.

Chester Arthur was 6'2" tall with reddish-brown hair and side-whiskers. He was considered a handsome man and an elegant dresser. He died on November 18, 1886 in New York City.

During Arthur's presidency (1881-1885)
 -The federal civil service system was reformed.
 -President Arthur called an international meeting
  to set standard time zones.

During 1881-1885:
 -Stories of adventure and suspense called dime
  novels were popular with kids.
 -Bank robber Jesse James was shot and killed.
 -New York and Chicago were connected by
  telephone lines.

GROVER CLEVELAND
(1885-1889) (1893-1897)

22 & 24

Born: March 18, 1837
Party: Democrat
Home state: New York
Terms of office: 1885-1889
1893-1897
Died: June 24, 1908

"I have tried so hard to do right."

Stephen Grover Cleveland was born March 18, 1837 in Caldwell, New Jersey. He stopped using Stephen as his first name when he was still a boy. Grover was one of nine children. His father was a Presbyterian minister with very strict rules. On Sundays the children were only allowed to go to church, read the Bible, and take quiet walks in the garden.

Grover left school at age 14. He went to work in a grocery store to help support his family. His father died when Grover was 16. Cleveland worked for two years at the New York Institution for the Blind. Then he worked on his uncle's farm. His uncle helped Grover find a job as a law clerk. Four years later he became a lawyer at the same company.

As a young lawyer Cleveland was active in the Democratic party. He was appointed assistant district attorney. In 1870 Cleveland was elected sheriff of Erie County. He personally hanged two convicted murders. He did not want to ask his deputies to do a job he wouldn't do himself. Cleveland won a reputation as an honest sheriff.

He returned to private practive as a lawyer after his term as sheriff. Cleveland was elected mayor of Buffalo in 1881 and governor of New York the following year. He was a strong governor who worked for reform in state government.

In the 1884 presidential election, government corruption was a major issue. The Republicans nominated James Blaine for president. Many people thought Blaine would do whatever big business wanted. Some Republicans even said they would vote for the Democratic candidate if he was an honest man. The Democrats nominated Cleveland. "Grover the Good" won the election with the support of many Republicans.

President Cleveland worked to reform the federal government. He made Cabinet appointments from both parties. He warned government departments to stop overspending. When Congress tried to pass laws to help special groups, Cleveland used his veto power. He vetoed more than 300 bills. He was a very hard worker as president. Often Cleveland worked at his desk till two or three o'clock in the morning.

On June 2, 1886, Cleveland became the only president to have a White House wedding. He married twenty-one-year-old Frances Folsom. He had been her guardian since the death of her father. Grover and Frances had five children. One of their daughters was the first child of a President born in the White House.

Cleveland ran for a second term in 1888. But he lost the election to Republican Benjamin Harrison. In 1892 Cleveland and Harrison were the presidential candidates again. This time Cleveland defeated Harrison.

Grover Cleveland is the only president to make a comeback after losing an election to a second term. Because Harrison was president between Cleveland's two terms, Cleveland is the only president with two numbers in the list of presidents. He was the twenty-second president and the twenty-fourth president.

During Cleveland's second administration, the U.S. economy was in serious trouble. Many people did not have jobs. There were strikes and riots. There was not enough gold in the U.S. Treasury. Many people blamed these problems on the President. He did not run for a third term.

Cleveland and his wife retired to Princeton, New Jersey. He spent his time writing and lecturing. He died June 24, 1908.

During Cleveland's first administration (1884-1889)
  -President Cleveland canceled the opening of Indian Territory and gave the land back to the Indians.
  -The first federal controls on business were passed by Congress.

83

During 1884-1889:
- The first box camera was sold.
- The Statue of Liberty was presented to the U.S. by the French government.

During Cleveland's second administration (1893-1897)
- The Panic of 1893 caused a stock market collapse.
- President Cleveland sent federal troops to Chicago to stop riots.

During 1893-1897:
- The first comic strip, "The Yellow Kid," was printed in a newspaper.
- The first professional football game was played.

PRESIDENTIAL NICKNAMES

Lincoln............................. Honest Abe
A. Johnson............................. Sir Veto
Grant .... "Uncle Sam" Grant
Hayes............................ Fraud President
Garfield...................... Preacher President
Arthur .... Gentleman Boss
Cleveland .... Uncle Jumbo

BENJAMIN HARRISON
(1889-1893)

23

Born: August 20, 1833
Party: Republican
Home state: Indiana
Term of office: 1889-1893
Died: March 13, 1901

"... So high a degree of prosperity and so general a diffusion of the comforts of life were never before enjoyed by our people ..."

Benjamin Harrison was born on August 20, 1833 in North Bend, Ohio. He was named for his great-grandfather who was a signer of the Declaration of Independence and a governor of Virginia. When Benjamin was seven his grandfather, William Henry Harrison, was elected president. The boy spent many hours at his grandfather's campaign headquarters.

Young Ben was one of nine children. Because there were no schools nearby, his father built a one-room log schoolhouse for his children. He hired a teacher to teach them reading, writing and arithmetic. Ben was an average student.

Harrison attended a college preparatory school and then Miami University in Ohio. He move to Cincinnati to study law. He married his college sweetheart, Caroline Scott. He was 19 and she was 20. They had a son and a daughter.

The Harrisons moved to Indianapolis where they lived in a boardinghouse. Ben worked as a lawyer. At the age of 27 he was elected reporter of the Supreme Court of Indiana. In the Civil War, Harrison was the colonel in charge of an Indiana volunteer regiment. He was promoted to brigadier general. After the war he returned to Indianapolis.

Harrison ran for governor of Indiana, but he lost the election. He served in the U.S. Senate from 1881-1887. The Republicans chose Harrison as their candidate for the 1888 election. The Democratic candidate was former President Cleveland.

Benjamin Harrison received 100,000 fewer votes than Cleveland. But Harrison was the winner in the Electoral College. Because Harrison did not receive a majority of the popular vote, he was called the "Minority President."

The Republicans were in control of Congress during Harrison's term. Congress voted pensions to any Civil War veteran who could not work. Congress also passed the Sherman Anti-trust Law to control big business.

Six new states were admitted to the U.S. during

Harrison's term. This brought the total number of states to 44. The country's population reached 63 million in 1890. And the Bureau of the Census reported that the nation was settled from coast to coast.

The White House was remodeled during Harrison's term. The President and First Lady did not like the new electric lights. Sometimes they let the lights burn all night because they were afraid to turn them off.

Harrison ran for re-election against Grover Cleveland in 1892. A few days before the election, Caroline Harrison died of tuberculosis. Harrison lost the election and returned to Indianapolis to practice law. At the age of 62 he married his wife's niece. They had one daughter. Benjamin Harrison died at age 67 at his home in Indianapolis.

During Harrison's presidency (1889-1893)
- The last major battle between Indians and U.S. troops took place at Wounded Knee Creek, South Dakota.
- Six more states were admitted: Washington, Idaho, Montana, Wyoming, North Dakota, and South Dakota.

During 1889-1893:
- *The Adventures of Sherlock Holmes* was published.
- The game of basketball was invented.
- Henry Ford made his first gasoline-powered car.

87

WILLIAM MCKINLEY
(1897-1901)

25

Born: January 29, 1843
Party: Republican
Home state: Ohio
Term of office: 1897-1901
Died: September 14, 1901

"I am a tariff man, standing on a tariff platform."

William McKinley was born on January 29, 1843 in Niles, Ohio. He was fond of school but he enjoyed the outdoors even more. As a boy his favorite game was "Old Sow." The object of the game was to knock a little block of wood into a hole in the ground. A curved stick was used to hit the block. The contest was somewhat like present-day golf. McKinley also enjoyed shooting marbles, making and flying kites, and shooting a bow and arrow.

William and his eight brothers and sisters went to a local private school. He continued his education at Allegheny College in Pennsylvania. After a year of college he taught school and worked in a post office.

He enlisted in the Ohio Volunteer Infantry at the beginning of the Civil War. William was made a mess sergeant. His job was serving hot meals to troops under fire. He served in several battles and was promoted to the rank of major.

After the Civil War McKinley worked as a law clerk and attended Albany Law School. He opened his own law office in Canton, Ohio. He married Ida Saxton, the daughter of a Canton banker.

In 1876 McKinley was elected to Congress. He served as a representative in the House for almost 15 years. He was elected governor of Ohio in 1891. The Republicans chose him as their candidate for president in 1896. He was the first president to campaign by telephone. McKinley telephoned his state campaign managers to give them instructions. He defeated William Jennings Bryan by more than half a million votes.

During McKinley's years in the White House, the U.S. gained large amounts of land. The Phillipines, Puerto Rico, Guam and Hawaii became U.S. territories. The "Open Door" policy was adopted during McKinley's term. This policy gave anyone who wanted to settle in the U.S. the right to do so. People from many different countries moved to the United States.

The island of Cuba became a new problem to the U.S. during McKinley's term. The Cubans had revolted against Spanish rule. The United States became involved when a U.S. battleship, the *Maine*, was blown up in

Havana Harbor. This led to the Spanish-American War.

McKinley was nominated for a second term in 1900. The President again defeated the Democratic candidate, William Jennings Bryan.

Ida, the President's wife, was an invalid. She had never recovered from the deaths of her two young daughters. The President received sympathy and respect for his kind treatment of his wife.

McKinley became the third president to be assassinated. On September 6, 1901, he was attending the Pan-American Exposition in Buffalo, New York. A man named Leon Czolgosz shot the President. McKinley died a few days later. Czolgosz was convicted of murder and electrocuted.

William McKinley was a stout 5'6" tall. He was a gentle man of great kindness. He liked to wear a white vest and a red carnation in his buttonhole.

During McKinley's presidency (1897-1901)
- The U.S. battleship *Maine* was blown up and sunk in Havana Harbor in Cuba.
- The Spanish-American War lasted less than four months.

During 1897-1901:
- The U.S. population was 76 million.
- Casey Jones, the famous engineer, was killed in a train wreck.
- The first automobile show was held.

THEODORE ROOSEVELT
(1901-1909)

26

Born: October 27, 1858
Party: Republican
Home state: New York
Term of office: 1901-1909
Died: January 6, 1919

"Speak softly and carry a big stick."

No president was ever more of an adventurer than Theodore Roosevelt. His hobbies were boxing, driving, exploring, hunting, mountain climbing, rowing, and wrestling.

Teddy Roosevelt was not healthy as a boy. He had asthma and bad eyesight. But he loved to read. His favorite books were adventure stories. He hoped someday to be like the characters in the books he read. He worked hard to build his body and his strength. Soon

Teddy could do more than any other boy his age.

He loved learning about animals, too. He made his bedroom into a taxidermist shop. He kept jars of chemicals for preserving animals all around the room. In the kitchen icebox he kept dead rats and squirrels fresh for mounting. Roosevelt even began writing a book when he was a boy. It was called "The Natural History of Insects" by Theodore Roosevelt, Jr.

Roosevelt entered Harvard College at the age of 18. He earned excellent grades and was elected to the national honor fraternity, Phi Beta Kappa. On his twenty-second birthday Teddy married his college sweetheart, Alice Lee. A year later he was elected to the New York state legislature. In 1884, Alice died after giving birth to their daughter. Theodore's mother died the same day.

Roosevelt went west to make a new life. He was a cowboy and rancher for three years. He rode horses, hunted buffalo, and even caught two thieves in the wildest part of the North Dakota Badlands.

After his life as a cowboy, Teddy Roosevelt returned to New York and ran for mayor. He lost that election. In 1895 he was appointed New York City's commissioner of police. During this time he married a childhood friend, Edith Carow. Both enjoyed the outdoors and sports of all kinds.

When the Spanish-American War was declared, Teddy was working for President Cleveland as Assistant Secretary of the Navy. He quit his job to join the Army as a lieutenant colonel. Roosevelt led the Rough Riders cavalry unit to victory in the famous charge up San Juan Hill in Cuba.

His fame helped make him governor of New York. But he made many enemies by taxing large corporations. His own party, the Republicans, feared his beliefs about "big business." They hoped to keep him in line by nominating him as McKinley's vice-president in 1900. As vice-president, Teddy would not have much power. And the Republicans could keep an eye on him.

Roosevelt had been vice-president for only six months when President McKinley was assassinated. Teddy had to come back from a camping trip to be sworn in as president. Many people were upset to see "that cowboy" in the White House.

President Roosevelt was known as the "Trust-Buster." He believed small businesses had to be protected from large corporations. He was afraid that large corporations would run the United States if they weren't kept under control.

Teddy always had time for his six children. They had free run of the White House. They gave parties, played ball in the East Room, and walked on stilts all over the White House. Roosevelt allowed his children to have many pets. Once the children wanted to cheer up their brother who was sick with the mumps. They shoved their pet pony in the White House elevator and took him to the third floor for a visit with the sick child. The President's favorite pet was a kangaroo rat that ate sugar at the breakfast table.

Roosevelt's exciting personality assured him a second term in the White House. He won easily in 1904. He probably could have been elected again in 1908. But he chose not to run for a third term. He wanted to go big game hunting in Africa instead. In 1912 Roosevelt decided to run for president again. He left the Republicans and formed his own party called the Progessive Party. Its popular name was the Bull Moose Party. Roosevelt received more votes than the Republicans but the Democrats won easily.

During his term as president, Roosevelt won the Nobel Peace Prize, added 125,000,000 acres to the national forests, and ordered the building of the Panama Canal. His policy of speaking softly and carrying a big stick explained the United States policy of keeping a large army and navy. He had great impact on U.S. foreign policy.

Teddy Roosevelt never lost his love of adventure. In 1914 Roosevelt went to explore the River of Doubt, deep in the Brazilian jungle. It almost cost him his life. One man from his party was eaten by piranha fish. Another lost his mind and killed a friend. For a while all the men had to eat were monkeys. Teddy caught malaria. He ran a fever of 105 degrees and pleaded to be left in the jungle to die. His men saved him and he returned home to a huge welcome.

Teddy Roosevelt was 5'10" tall. He was known for his heavy mustache and glasses that clipped on his nose. He had a high-pitched voice and gritted his teeth when he smiled. Roosevelt, the most colorful of our presidents, died January 6, 1919 on Long Island, New York.

During Roosevelt's presidency (1901-1909)
- Construction of the Panama Canal was started.
- Oklahoma became a state.
- The government began regulating big business.

During 1901-1909:
- The first World Series of baseball was played.
- The Wright brothers made the first successful airplane flight.
- Teddy bears were a popular new toy named after President Roosevelt.

PRESIDENTIAL NAME GAME

Can you unscramble these names?

NAV RENBU	___ _____
KOPL	____
TRGAN	_____
LANDLCEVE	_____
SEYHA	_____
NILCONL	_____
NANAHCUB	_____
LEYMCNIK	_____
THURRA	_____
NOSKAJC	_____
RELYT	_____
FEIDLRAG	_____
CEREIP	_____
LLIFEMOR	_____
LORTYA	_____

WILLIAM TAFT
(1909-1913)

27

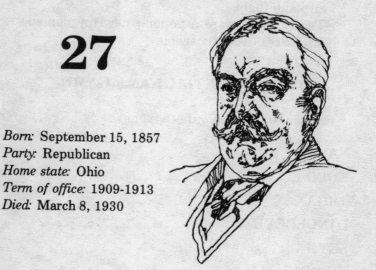

Born: September 15, 1857
Party: Republican
Home state: Ohio
Term of office: 1909-1913
Died: March 8, 1930

"Politics, when I am in it, makes me sick."

William Taft was the heaviest president. He weighed 325 pounds when he was elected president. Many people have heard stories that Taft once got stuck in the White House bathtub. This story is not true. Actually, Taft had a special bathtub installed in the White House. It was so large that four normal-sized men could fit in it comfortably.

Young Willie Taft was an excellent baseball player. He played catcher and was a tremendous hitter. Taft was a good wrestler, too.

He did well in all his classes. Taft went to college at Yale and graduated second in his class. He went on to law school in Cincinnati. In 1886 Taft married Helen Herron. He worked as a lawyer and then became a judge. He and his wife had three children.

Taft never wanted to be president. He wished all his life to be a Supreme Court justice. He hoped that the appointments he got from presidents would finally lead him to his goal.

Teddy Roosevelt liked Taft. He said he had never seen a better administrator. He sent Taft to the Philippines to be its first governor. There, Taft had roads and public schools built. He also set up a system of government that allowed the Philippinos to govern themselves. President Roosevelt later made Taft his Secretary of War. When the Panama Canal was built, Taft was there supervising the men and construction.

When Roosevelt chose not to run in 1908 for president, he asked Taft to run. Taft's wife added to the pressure. Taft finally agreed to run. He did not like the idea. But he felt he should serve his country in whatever way it needed him. With Roosevelt's support, Taft won easily.

While Taft was president, Arizona and New Mexico were added to the Union. The United States then had 48 states. Taft continued Roosevelt's policy of cracking down on big business.

Taft had many firsts as president. He was the first president to take up golf as a hobby. He was the first president to make $75,000 a year for his services. He was also the first and only president to drive around Washington in an electric car. Taft was the only president to later serve as Chief Justice of the U.S. Supreme Court.

Taft died March 8, 1930.

During Taft's presidency (1909-1913)
- The presidential Oval Office was added to the White House.
- Arizona and New Mexico became states.
- President Taft urged Congress to pass an income tax law.

During 1909-1913:
- Fingerprints were first used as evidence in court cases.
- Edgar Rice Burroughs wrote *Tarzan of the Apes.*
- Henry Ford used the first assembly lines to produce Model-T Fords.

WOODROW WILSON
(1913-1921)

28

Born: December 28, 1856
Party: Democratic
Home state: New Jersey
Term of office: 1913-1921
Died: February 3, 1924

"A Yankee always thinks he's right.
A Scotch-Irish knows it."

Woodrow Wilson was born on December 28, 1856, in Staunton, Virginia. He was a little boy during the Civil War years. When he grew up, he could remember having seen General Robert E. Lee and Jefferson Davis.

Wilson went to Princeton College and the University of Virginia law school. Then he earned a Ph.D. in political science from Johns Hopkins University. Wilson was the most highly educated man ever to become president.

He was a man of many interests. He wrote several books on history and politics. He loved the theater. He played golf. And he was a good singer.

Woodrow Wilson became a college professor in 1885. During the same year he married Ellen Axson. She was a talented artist from Georgia.

Wilson taught at three different colleges in the next few years. At one school, he also coached the football team. During these years the Wilsons had three daughters.

At the age of 45 Wilson became president of Princeton College. He later became governor of New Jersey. He was elected president of the U.S. in 1912.

As president, Wilson helped get some important reforms passed in Congress. These laws helped to keep banks and business under control. Wilson called his ideas the New Freedom.

Mrs. Wilson helped poor people. She sold some of her paintings and gave the money to charity. She also asked Congress to pass a law for better housing for the poor in Washington.

Ellen Wilson died in the White House in 1914. A year later the President married a widow, Edith Galt. In later years she was called "Mrs. President."

In 1916 Wilson was re-elected to the presidency. During this term, the U.S. entered World War I. Wilson was a strong leader during the war. He wrote a famous plan for peace, the Fourteen Points. This called for all nations to work together for peace. A group called the League of Nations would be formed. Then countries could solve their problems by talking instead of fighting.

Many countries thought the League of Nations was a good idea. But the American people were tired of sharing the problems of other nations. The public did not accept the idea.

President Wilson went on an 8,000 mile speaking tour for the League of Nations. His doctors said he was not strong enough for this tour. They were right. President Wilson had a stroke that paralyzed his left side. He was very sick and could not continue his duties as president.

Normally, the vice-president would have taken over the president's job. But Vice-President Thomas Marshall didn't want the job of president. Marshall was most famous for his quote, "What this country needs is a good 5¢ cigar." No one in Washington wanted a man like Marshall to lead the country.

The only other person who knew enough about Wilson's ideas was his wife Edith. She always sat in on his private conferences. She was the only other person who knew the codes used to send messages to generals in Europe. While the president was paralyzed, Edith made all the executive decisions. Cabinet members and Senate leaders listened to her. Many believe that Wilson's success as president was due partly to Edith.

Wilson was never again in good health. But he recovered enough to act as president again. In 1920 the Nobel Peace Prize was awarded to President Wilson for his peace efforts.

He died three years after leaving the White House. His dying words were "I'm a broken man, but I'm ready."

During Wilson's presidency (1913-1921)
  -The Panama Canal opened.
  -The United States entered World War I.

-Wilson was the first president to visit Europe
while in office.

During 1913-1921:
-*Tarzan of the Apes* was published.
-The first movies with sound were issued.
-A new Model-T Ford cost $360 in 1917.

MATCH GAME

Match the first and last names of these presidents.

ABRAHAM	WILSON
JAMES	HAYES
THEODORE	ARTHUR
ZACHARY	VAN BUREN
FRANKLIN	TAYLOR
ULYSSES	LINCOLN
JOHN	ROOSEVELT
GROVER	JACKSON
THOMAS	FILLMORE
MILLARD	PIERCE
MARTIN	CLEVELAND
WOODROW	JEFFERSON
RUTHERFORD	POLK
CHESTER	GRANT
ANDREW	TYLER

WARREN G. HARDING
(1921-1923)

29

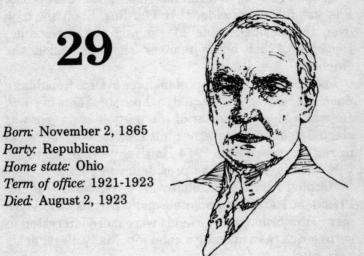

Born: November 2, 1865
Party: Republican
Home state: Ohio
Term of office: 1921-1923
Died: August 2, 1923

"I am not fit for this office
and never should have been here."

Warren Gamaliel Harding was the oldest of eight
children. His family lived on a farm in Ohio. Warren had
a job with a small newspaper when he was a boy. He
helped set type and run the press. When he was 14
Warren went to Ohio Central College where he was
editor of the school yearbook. He graduated when he
was 17.

Harding tried teaching in a country school. He left

after one term and rejoined his family in Marion, Ohio. Harding and two friends bought a daily newspaper, the *Marion Star*. A weekly subscription was ten cents.

At the age of 25 Warren married Florence DeWolfe. She was five years older than Harding. Soon she took over the business side of running the newspaper. Because of her bossy manner she was called the Duchess.

The *Star* became an important force in Ohio Republican politics. Harding was elected to the state senate in 1899. He was a loyal supporter of the party leaders. He was elected lieutenant governor but lost the election when he ran for governor. In 1914 Harding was elected to the U.S. Senate. He won the presidency in 1920.

Harding's term was filled with gossip and scandal. President Harding appointed many friends to government jobs. Some of his friends were more interested in getting rich than in doing a good job. Many illegal deals were made.

In 1923 news of these scandals started to leak out. Two government officals committed suicide because they could not face being caught for their crimes. Harding decided to go on a cross-country good-will tour. The President became ill and died in San Francisco on August 2, 1923.

Some people think Harding was poisoned so he couldn't testify against his friends. Mrs. Harding refused to allow an autopsy. She burned President Harding's papers and letters. Many facts about Harding will never be known.

Warren was a handsome man. He was six feet tall and had blue eyes. Harding played the cornet as a hobby. He also chewed tobacco.

During Harding's presidency (1921-1923)
- President Harding called the Washington Conference for the Limitation of Armament. This was a meeting of many countries to work for peace.
- Harding appointed a budget director for the federal government.

During 1921-1923:
- People listened to the new jazz music played on the newest addition to the home—the radio.
- Short skirts were fashionable.
- King Tut's tomb was discovered by archaeologists.

TRIVIA TIME

Who are the four presidents shown on Mt. Rushmore?

_____

_____

_____

_____

CALVIN COOLIDGE
(1923-1929)

30

Born: July 4, 1872
Party: Republican
Home state: Massachusetts
Term of office: 1923-1929
Died: January 5, 1933

"The business of America is business."

Calvin Coolidge was born July 4, 1872 at Plymouth Notch, Vermont. He was the only president born on Independence Day. As a boy he worked on the family farm across from his father's store. His grandfather gave him his own farm when Cal was only six years old.

He loved to ride horseback as a child. He was so good he could ride his horse standing up like a circus performer. Calvin attended private schools and graduated from Amherst College with honors in 1895. He worked as a law clerk so he could become a lawyer.

Coolidge became interested in politics. He was first elected to the Northampton, Massachusetts city council in 1899. In the next few years he won respect as the best Republican campaign manager in the state. Coolidge was elected to the Massachusetts House of Representatives in 1906. Then he became mayor of Northampton in 1910. He served one term. Coolidge continued to be a winner. He won the race for the Massachusetts state senate in 1912. Coolidge became lieutenant governor in 1916 and governor of Massachusetts in 1919.

As governor he won national praise. The police department in Boston had gone on strike. Coolidge said, "There is no right to strike against the public safety by anybody, anywhere, any time!" He ordered the police back to work. The police refused. He sent in the state militia to force the police back to work. Everyone in the country, including the President, praised Coolidge. He was re-elected governor by a record margin.

In 1920 Coolidge was nominated to run on the Republican ticket as vice-president. Warren Harding was the presidential candidate. Harding and Coolidge won the election of 1920. Coolidge had put together a long string of political victories.

At 2:30 A.M. on August 3, 1923, Coolidge learned of President Harding's death. The Vice-President was visiting his father on the family farm when he heard the news. Coolidge's father, a notary public, gave the oath of office to his son. The United States had a new president.

The 1920s was a time of growth for this country. The decade was called the Roaring Twenties. People loved this era of fun and easy living. No one thought the good times would ever come to an end.

Coolidge was re-elected in 1924 because the country was doing so well. The citizens were content. Coolidge limited immigration. He made the nations the U.S. had helped in World War I pay back the money they had borrowed. Coolidge also cut taxes for citizens who made big salaries. Each new policy made someone happy.

Tragedy struck the White House with the death of Coolidge's younger son, Calvin, Jr. The boy died from blood poisoning developed from a blister.

President Coolidge was known as Silent Cal. He never said more than he had to. Once at a Washington party, a guest started to talk to him. She told Coolidge she had bet that she could get the President to say more than two words. Silent Cal looked at her and said, "You lose." In 1927 he held a news conference. He handed each reporter a note that said only, "I do not choose to run for president in 1928."

Coolidge spent his retirement at home in Northampton where he wrote his autobiography. He died January 5, 1933.

During Coolidge's presidency (1923-1929)
  -President Coolidge appointed a special prosecutor to investigate the scandals of Harding's
   presidency.
  -Congress passed a bonus bill for World War I
   veterans over Coolidge's veto.
  -The Kellogg-Briand Pact to outlaw war was
   signed by 23 nations.

During 1923-1929:
- Mickey Mouse appeared in his first movie, *Steamboat Willie.*
- Charles Lindbergh flew his plane, *The Spirit of St. Louis,* from New York to Paris.
- The latest dance was the Charleston.

FOURTH OF JULY FACTS

1. Only one president was born on July 4. Can you name him? _____

2. Three presidents died on the Fourth of July. Who are they? _____

   _____

   _____

3. Who was president on July 4, 1876, when the U.S. celebrated its 100th birthday?

   _____

HERBERT HOOVER
(1929-1933)

31

Born: August 10, 1874
Party: Republican
Home state: California
Term of office: 1929-1933
Died: October 20, 1964

"Prosperity is just around the corner."

Herbert Hoover was born on August 10, 1874 in a small town in Iowa. Both his parents died before Herbert was nine. He went to live with his aunt and uncle in Oregon. As a boy Herbert liked to invent things. Once he and his cousin used an old saw to make a mowing machine. The two boys also made a molasses mill out of an old clothes wringer.

Herbert attended a private Quaker school where he received an excellent education. At 15 he went to work as an office boy in a real estate business. Hoover met several engineers there. He decided he wanted to be an engineer, too. Hoover worked his way through Stanford University in California.

After graduation Hoover became a very successful engineer. He managed gold mines in Australia. He was the chief engineer of China's bureau of mines. He started his own engineering company and traveled all over the world supervising projects. Hoover was a millionaire by the age of 40.

Hoover's wife, Lou, was also very interested in minerals and mining. She went on all of Hoover's business trips. They had two children whom they also took along on their travels. By the time he was four years old, Herbert, Jr., had circled the globe three times.

Hoover started working for the U.S. government during World War I. As U.S. Food Administrator, he helped get food distributed to all parts of the country. He also worked in Europe to help distribute food there. His war work made him famous in the U.S.

He served as Secretary of Commerce for Presidents Harding and Coolidge. Hoover reorganized the Department of Commerce. He also helped reduce the working day from twelve to eight hours.

The Republicans chose Hoover as their presidential candidate in 1928. The Democratic nominee was Governor Al Smith of New York. Hoover did not do much campaigning. But he won the election by a landslide.

Seven months after Hoover became president the stock market collapsed. The country entered the "Great Depression." The American people had been promised "a chicken in every pot and a car in every garage." Now

111

the people needed someone to blame for this disaster. They blamed President Hoover. Shantytowns sprang up across the nation. They were called Hoovervilles. Broken-down automobiles hauled by mules were called Hoover-Wagons. Hoover Flags was the name given to empty pockets turned inside out.

Hoover tried to help the situation. But as his party said, "He did too little, too late." He set up the Reconstruction Finance Corporation that loaned money to businesses and homeowners. But he did not believe in federal aid to the unemployed. Hoover's name was still stamped on the Depression. President Hoover ran for a second term. But Franklin D. Roosevelt won by a landslide.

Herbert Hoover was 5'11". He had broad shoulders and a round face. He was a stickler for details and a workaholic. After leaving the presidency Hoover wrote several books. One of his books was about Woodrow Wilson. He was the first president to write a book about another president.

Hoover died October 20, 1964 in New York City at the age of 90.

During Hoover's presidency (1929-1933)
-The stock market crashed in October, 1929.
-The Great Depression caused many banks and businesses to fail.
-Thirteen million Americans could not find jobs.

During 1929-1933:
-The first Nancy Drew book was published.
-The first regularly-issued comic book, *Famous*

Funnies, sold for ten cents.
-Popular songs were "Who's Afraid of the Big Bad Wolf?" and "Brother, Can You Spare a Dime?"

FRANKLIN D. ROOSEVELT
(1933-1945)

32

Born: January 30, 1882
Party: Democratic Party
Home state: New York
Term of office: 1933-1945
Died: April 12, 1945

"The only thing we have to fear is fear itself."

Franklin Roosevelt had everything a child could want. All his ancestors were rich, famous, or beautiful. His fifth cousin was President Theodore Roosevelt. Franklin's parents were wealthy. He grew up on a 187-acre estate in Hyde Park, New York. At the age of four he owned his own pony. At 16 Franklin had his own 21-foot sailboat. He was educated by tutors and at boarding schools. He toured Europe eight times before he was 16.

During college Franklin was editor of the *Harvard*

Crimson, the school's newspaper. He bought a lithograph machine to print the newspaper. On the day of the machine's first use, Harvard was playing Yale in football. As the fans left the stadium, they received copies of the *Crimson.* The score of the Harvard-Yale game was already in the paper.

Roosevelt was not an outstanding student. After graduation from Harvard, he attended Columbia Law School. He dropped out after failing several classes. But he had learned enough to pass the bar exam and become a lawyer. Franklin married a distant cousin, Eleanor Roosevelt, in 1905.

He began his political career in 1910. In Roosevelt's district, no Democrat had won a state senate seat in 54 years. But Roosevelt carried on a person-to-person campaign and pulled off an upset victory in the election. In 1912 Roosevelt supported Woodrow Wilson for president. When Wilson won the election, he appointed Roosevelt Assistant Secretary of the Navy. In 1920 Roosevelt was picked by the Democrats to run as James Cox's vice-presidential candidate. They lost the election to Warren Harding. But Roosevelt had won national fame during the campaign.

In 1921 Roosevelt was vacationing at the family's summer home in Canada. He awoke one day and could not move his legs. He had caught polio. He would never regain complete use of his legs.

While Roosevelt was recovering from polio, he wrote a movie script based on the story of the ship "Old Ironsides." No one in Hollywood bought the script. He tried to work on other projects, too. One was the development of an inter-city "blimp" line. No one bought that idea, either.

Roosevelt worked hard to recover from his polio attack. He learned to use crutches and a wheel chair. He had to wear braces on his legs.

In 1928 he was elected governor of New York. While he was governor, the stock market crashed and the Depression began. In 1932 the Democratic party nominated Roosevelt for president. He was the first presidential candidate to deliver his acceptance speech in person. He promised the American people a New Deal. His campaign song was "Happy Days Are Here Again." Roosevelt won the election by a landslide.

President Roosevelt worked hard to bring the country out of the Depression. He believed the government had a duty to help its people. His program was named the New Deal. One part of the New Deal was called the Works Progress Administration (WPA). The WPA hired men and women to build roads, bridges, and dams. They remodeled government buildings and built new ones. The WPA even hired out-of-work artists to paint murals inside public buildings.

The Civilian Conservation Corps (CCC) was a program to provide jobs for unemployed young men. They planted trees, built dams, and fought forest fires. More than two million men served in the CCC from 1933-1945.

Social Security was another part of the New Deal. Roosevelt believed each citizen had a right to a steady income when he retired. Workers would pay a little to Social Security each week. Then they would have a monthly income after retirement.

One of the biggest projects of the New Deal was the

Tennessee Valley Authority (TVA). Roosevelt thought that people should have control over the power company in their own area. The TVA is a power company that is owned by all the people who use its electricity. The New Deal changed America. Most New Deal policies are still in effect today.

Roosevelt was president during most of World War II. He was a fine leader during this time of crisis. People across the country listened to their radios during Roosevelt's "Fireside Chats." He kept the country calm while war raged in Europe. He asked all Americans to help in the war effort. Victory gardens, ration coupons, and meatless meals were ways of helping. Women went to work in factories. Around the clock the shipyards, factories, and steel mills were busy.

Franklin Roosevelt was not the only politician in the family. His wife, Eleanor, was active in politics, too. Her political career began when she campaigned for Roosevelt after his polio attack. When Roosevelt was elected president, Eleanor traveled to Europe on fact-finding missions. She helped poor children and worked for equal rights for minority groups. She wrote a daily newspaper column and four books. She also served as a delegate to the United Nations.

Roosevelt was the first president to appoint a woman to his cabinet. He was the only handicapped president. He was the only president to be elected to four terms. He was also the first president to appear on television.

President Roosevelt died April 12, 1945 in Warm Springs, Georgia. He was posing for a portrait when he said, "I have a terrific headache." Moments later he was dead.

Roosevelt was 6'2" tall and weighed 190 pounds. His trademarks were a wide grin, a cigarette holder, and a black cape.

During Roosevelt's presidency (1933-1945)
  -Prohibition ended.
  -The Depression left many people without jobs or homes.
  -Pearl Harbor was attacked by the Japanese and the U.S. entered World War II.

During 1933-1945:
  -The first Superman comic was printed.
  -Walt Disney's movie, *The Three Little Pigs,* won an Academy Award.
  -Jesse Owens won four gold medals at the Olympics in Germany.
  -Regular television broadcasts started.

HOME STATES

Seventeen presidents came from 3 states—New York, Virginia, and Ohio.

NEW YORK

_____   _____

_____   _____

_____   _____

VIRGINIA

_____   _____

_____   _____

_____

OHIO

_____   _____

_____   _____

_____   _____

HARRY S. TRUMAN
(1945-1953)

33

Born: May 8, 1884
Party: Democratic
Home state: Missouri
Term of office: 1945-1953
Died: December 26, 1972

"The buck stops here."

"S" is Harry Truman's middle initial, but it does not stand for a name. When he was born his parents could not decide on a middle name for him. They did not know which of Harry's grandfathers to honor. Harry ended up with simply S.

As a child Harry loved to read. By the time he was fourteen he had finished reading all the books in the Independence, Missouri library. He also took piano lessons. At one time Truman was interested in a career as a musician.

After high school he went to work to help support his family. He learned many skills from all the different jobs he held. He was a timekeeper for a railroad, a mailroom clerk for the *Kansas City Star*, a bookkeeper, a bank clerk, a road overseer, and a postmaster. He also ran the family farm for eleven years.

Truman wanted to enter West Point. But he was turned down because of his poor eyesight. He volunteered for the army when the U.S. entered World War I.

During the war in France, Captain Truman was often in the thick of battle. Many times bullets buzzed only inches from his head. The men Truman led thought he had some kind of protective power. They would volunteer to go wherever Truman went. They thought that if they were with him they would be safe.

When he returned from the war, Truman married his long-time sweetheart, Bess Wallace. They had first met in Sunday School class when they were six years old. Bess always thought it was funny that Harry took so many years to propose to her.

Bess was an athlete. In high school, she was a champion shot putter and basketball player. She was also good at tennis and ping-pong. Harry and Bess had one daughter, Margaret.

Truman became a partner in a men's clothing store. But the store did not have enough business, and it closed.

In 1922 Truman entered local politics in Kansas City. Tom Pendergast was in charge of the Democratic Party in Kansas City. He helped Truman win election to a county job. Truman also attended law school at night but did not receive a degree.

Harry Truman was elected to the U.S. Senate in 1934. He was re-elected in 1940. By this time, he was becoming well-known. In 1944 he became Roosevelt's running mate. Roosevelt was re-elected to a fourth term, and Truman became Vice-President.

But Truman served as Vice-President for only eighty-two days. President Roosevelt died in Warm Springs, Georgia, and Harry S. Truman became the thirty-third president. He was the first president to take office in the midst of a war.

Soon after Truman became President, the United Nations was formed. This group of nations would work for peace throughout the world.

But World War II was still going on. Germany soon surrendered. The Allies and Japan were still at war.

President Truman had to make a very hard decision. He decided to drop the atomic bomb on two cities in Japan. Many people still disagree over whether Truman made the best choice. The atomic bomb led to the surrender of Japan and the end of World War II. But it also was the beginning of the Atomic Age.

After the war there were new problems with wage and price controls and inflation. There were strikes by some labor unions. At Truman's order, the government took control for a short time of the railroads and coal mines.

In 1948 Truman ran for re-election against Governor Thomas Dewey of New York. Everyone thought Truman would lose. On election night the *Chicago Daily Tribune* headline read DEWEY DEFEATS TRUMAN. Later President Truman held up that newspaper with a big smile because *he* had won the election!

In 1950 Truman was faced with another hard decision.

Communist North Korea invaded South Korea. The U.S. entered the Korean War.

Truman was a hard worker as President. He often woke up at 5:30 and worked a sixteen-hour day on the problems of the country.

During most of Truman's second term, he and his family didn't live in the White House. It was being completely remodeled. The Truman family lived across the street in Blair House. On November 1, 1950, two men tried to shoot their way into Blair House and kill the President. One guard was killed before the men were captured. The President was not hurt.

Harry and Bess returned to Independence in 1953. They were one of the few presidential couples to celebrate their fiftieth wedding anniversary. President Truman died in 1972. He is buried in the courtyard of the Truman Library in Independence, Missouri.

During Truman's presidency (1945-1953):
 -The United Nations was formed.
 -World War II ended.
 -North Atlantic Treaty Organization (NATO) was formed.

During 1945-1953:
 -The first computer was built.
 -The first electric blankets were sold.
 -Bikini bathing suits were the newest style.

DWIGHT D. EISENHOWER
(1953-1961)

34

Born: October 14, 1890
Party: Republican
Home state: Kansas
Term of office: 1953-1961
Died: March 28, 1969

"You know, once in a while I get to the point, with
everybody staring at me, where I want to go back
indoors and pull down the curtains."

Dwight David Eisenhower was born in Denison,
Texas in 1890. His family moved back to Kansas when
he was still a baby. Dwight and his five brothers worked
at odd jobs to help support the family.

He almost lost his leg as a child. Dwight developed
blood poisoning from a cut in his leg. The doctor wanted
to amputate the leg. But Dwight and his family said no
and the leg healed.

In high school Dwight picked up the nickname Ike. He wanted to go to college, but his parents couldn't afford to send him. So he entered the U.S. Military Academy at West Point. He played on the football team until he broke his knee. He was an average student.

After his graduation the army sent Ike to Texas. There he met Mamie Doud. They were married in 1916.

During World War I, Eisenhower was an instructor at military camps. At one camp he was in charge of training men to use tanks. The job was hard because they didn't have any real tanks for practice. Eisenhower did a good job anyway.

He went on to serve in the Panama Canal Zone. Then Ike attended the Army General Staff School in Kansas. He graduated first in his class of 275 officers. Next he attended the War College in Washington, D.C. He then served on the staff of the Assistant Secretary of War.

In 1932 he became an aide to General Douglas MacArthur. Later Eisenhower served in the Phillipines for four years.

World War II brought a new need for experienced officers. Eisenhower rose from lieutenant colonel to commanding general of the European Theater of Operations. He commanded the invasions of French North Africa, Sicily, and Italy. Then, President Roosevelt appointed Eisenhower Supreme Commander of all the Allied forces in Europe. General Eisenhower was in charge of the D-Day invasion of France.

By the time the war ended, Eisenhower was the most popular soldier in the U.S. and abroad. He became Chief of Staff of the U.S. Army after the war. He wrote a book called *Crusade in Europe*. It told about his World

War II service. His book was a best seller.

In 1948 Eisenhower became president of Columbia University. Both the Democrats and the Republicans wanted him to run for U.S. president. But Eisenhower said no to these offers.

General Eisenhower returned to the army in 1950 as Supreme Commander of NATO. Then in 1952, Ike accepted the Republican nomination for president. Senator Richard Nixon was his vice-presidential running mate.

The American people liked Eisenhower. He had a fatherly image and a happy grin. People wore campaign buttons that said, "I Like Ike." He was elected in a landslide victory.

President Eisenhower worked to keep peace at home and in other countries. He helped to end the Korean War. He sent U.S. Marines to help keep peace in Lebanon. He worked for peaceful uses of atomic energy.

His worldwide goodwill tour helped other countries understand the U.S. Ike traveled 320,000 miles and visited 27 countries.

Eisenhower also worked on problems in this country. Federal troops were sent to protect black students in Arkansas. A huge highway building program was started. Better benefits were given to retired people.

Ike had three serious illnesses while he was president. He had a heart attack in 1955. Then he had an emergency operation the next year. In 1957 Eisenhower had a mild stroke.

Many people thought Ike wouldn't run for a second term because of his health. But he did run again in 1956. He won another landslide victory. He was only the second Republican president to serve two four-year terms.

Eisenhower was a president with many hobbies. He liked to play golf and bridge. He watched movies in the White House theater and read Western novels. He also enjoyed painting, cooking, and fishing.

The Eisenhowers had one son, John. He became an army officer like his father. The President loved to play with his four grandchildren. His grandson, David Eisenhower, later married Julie Nixon. Her father was Ike's vice-president.

After leaving the White House Ike and Mamie retired to their farm near Gettysburg, Pennsylvania. Eisenhower wrote two books about his years as president.

He died of heart failure in 1969. Ike was buried at his boyhood home in Kansas.

During Eisenhower's presidency (1953-1961)
  -Military advisers and supplies were sent to help South Vietnam.
  -The first seven astronauts were selected.
  -Hawaii and Alaska became states.

During 1953-1961:
  -The minimum wage became $1 an hour.
  -A polio vaccine was developed.
  -Teenagers wore bobby socks, drove hot rods, and listened to rock and roll music.

JOHN F. KENNEDY
(1961-1963)

35

Born: May 29, 1917
Party: Democratic
Home state: Massachusetts
Term of office: 1961-1963
Died: November 22, 1963

"Ask not what your country can do for you;
ask what you can do for your country."

John Fitzgerald Kennedy was the youngest man ever elected president. He was the first Roman Catholic president. And he was the first president born in the twentieth century.

He was the second of nine children. His nickname was Jack. His father was very wealthy. Each of the Kennedy children inherited a million dollars at the age of twenty-one.

John and his brothers and sisters liked sports. They played tennis and touch football. They swam at their home in Palm Beach. They sailed at their summer home in Hyannis Port, Massachusetts. Their father taught them to play to win. Second best was never good enough.

After sixth grade, John attended private schools. He was an average student. He went on to college at Harvard.

During his college years, Kennedy visited England where his father was U.S. Ambassador. There Kennedy saw changes in pre-war Europe. In his senior year he began studying politics. He became a serious student.

In the fall of 1939 Kennedy injured his back playing football. While he was recovering, he wrote a long paper for school. It was about England just before World War II. His teachers thought the paper was excellent. Kennedy graduated from Harvard with honors, mainly because of his writing.

Kennedy kept working on the paper after graduation. He made it into a book called *Why England Slept.* It was a best seller soon after it was published.

In the spring of 1941 Kennedy tried to enlist in the Army. He was turned down because of his back injury. He did exercises to strengthen his back and enlisted in the Navy. He was given command of a patrol torpedo (PT) boat in the South Pacific.

One night in August 1943, Kennedy almost lost his life. He and his crew were on patrol in PT 109. A Japanese destroyer rammed the PT boat and cut it in half. Two crew members were killed. Others were hurt. Kennedy reinjured his back. The men were in the water for fifteen hours. Kennedy saved one injured man by holding the man's life jacket strap in his teeth. Finally they reached a small island. They were rescued a few days later. Kennedy was given a medal for his actions.

After he was discharged from the Navy, Kennedy became a newspaper reporter. Then he decided to enter politics. He ran for the House of Representatives in 1946. The whole Kennedy family helped in the campaign and Kennedy won. He was re-elected twice.

In 1952 Kennedy was elected to the Senate. His campaign manager was his younger brother, Robert. John Kennedy became the leading Democrat from Massachusetts.

Senator Kennedy married Jacqueline Bouvier in September 1953. They had a huge wedding with 900 guests.

A few months later Kennedy had two operations on his back. While he was recovering, he wrote another book, *Profiles in Courage*. This book was a best seller and won the Pulitzer Prize.

In 1960 Kennedy ran against Richard Nixon for president. Once again, his brother Robert ran his campaign. The Kennedy family worked hard to help John win. The two candidates had four debates on national television. That was the first time that most of the American people could see and hear the candidates giving their views. Kennedy won by the closest margin ever in a presidential election.

During Kennedy's term, the White House buzzed with activity. Jackie Kennedy loved to give parties and dinners. She invited musicians and dancers to perform at the White House. She had many rooms in the White House remodeled. And she was the hostess for a TV tour of the White House.

President Kennedy had many new ideas. He called these ideas the New Frontier. He wanted more civil rights laws and more money for schools. He started two volunteer groups, VISTA and the Peace Corps. Kennedy also helped get the U.S. space program started. He promised that by the end of the decade an American would walk on the moon.

There were some serious problems with other countries during Kennedy's term. One problem was called the Bay of Pigs. This is the name of a small bay in Cuba. Another crisis was the building of the Berlin Wall in East Germany. The most serious problem was the Cuban Missile Crisis. The Soviet Union installed missiles on Cuba. President Kennedy insisted that the Soviet Union remove the missiles. Through each of these crises, Kennedy showed he was a strong leader.

President Kennedy was an interesting man. He liked sitting in rocking chairs because it made his back feel better. He believed in physical fitness. He hated to wear hats. He didn't like it when strangers touched him. He loved watching movies, especially Westerns and Civil War films.

Kennedy's favorite part of the day was the hour when his children, Caroline and John, Jr., played in the President's Oval Office. The children had many pets: five dogs, a cat, two birds, and two hamsters. They also had three ponies named Tex, Macaroni, and Leprechaun.

John F. Kennedy was the fourth president to be assassinated in office. On November 22, 1963, he was shot in Dallas, Texas. Lee Harvey Oswald was accused of the murder. Two days later Oswald was shot to death by Jack Ruby at the Dallas police station.

There are many unanswered questions about Kennedy's assassination. Many people think others were involved in the murder in addition to Oswald. Kennedy's death has been the subject of many books and investigations. But the whole truth may never be known.

During Kennedy's presidency (1961-1963)
- The Peace Corps was created.
- Alan Shepard became the first American astronaut to make a space flight.
- John Glenn was the first American to orbit the earth.

During 1961-1963:
- The first Barbie dolls were sold.
- Skateboarding was the newest outdoor sport.
- The Twist was the most popular dance.

COLLEGE QUIZ

1. Which president founded a university and designed its buildings? _____

2. Which college graduated the most presidents?
   _____

3. Which U.S. presidents were also college presidents?
   _____
   _____
   _____
   _____

4. Which presidents didn't attend college?
   _____
   _____
   _____
   _____
   _____
   _____
   _____
   _____

LYNDON B. JOHNSON
(1963-1969)

36

Born: August 27, 1908
Party: Democratic
Home state: Texas
Term of office: 1963-1969
Died: January 22, 1973

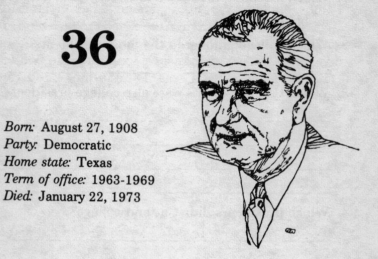

"Let us reason together."

Lyndon Baines Johnson was born on a Texas ranch in 1908. His parents had both been teachers. His father and grandfather had served in the Texas legislature. Lyndon grew up to be a teacher and politician, too.

Lyndon and his family moved to a small town named for his grandfather—Johnson City, Texas. The family didn't have much money. So Lyndon did odd jobs to earn spending money. He shined shoes, picked cotton, and worked for a road building crew.

After high school he and some friends hitchhiked to California. Lyndon worked as a fruit picker, dishwasher, and handy man. He returned to Texas and worked his way through Southwest Texas State Teachers College.

Johnson taught public speaking at Sam Houston High School for a year. Then he moved to Washington to work as a secretary for a Texas congressman. That job was the beginning of Johnson's long career in politics.

On a trip home to Texas, Lyndon met Lady Bird Taylor. He asked her to marry him on their first date. Two months later they were married. Several years later, Lady Bird used her inheritance to buy a Texas radio station and a TV station. Her investments grew into a multimillion-dollar fortune.

Johnson was elected to the U.S. House of Representatives in 1937. He did such a good job that no one ran against him in the next three elections.

During World War II, Johnson was the first member of Congress to go on active military duty. He served in the Navy and received a Silver Star for gallantry under enemy fire. Lady Bird helped run his congressional office during this time.

Johnson made his second try for the Senate in 1948. He had lost an earlier election in 1941. This time the Democratic primary was so close that a runoff election was held. Johnson won by only 87 votes. He went on to win the Senate seat.

At 44, Senator Johnson became the youngest Senate Democratic floor leader ever. He worked hard on civil rights laws. He was good at getting Democrats and Republicans together. In 1955 Johnson had a heart attack. His wife again helped run his office until he was able to get back to work.

Johnson wanted to become the Democratic presidential candidate in 1960. But he settled for being Kennedy's running mate. Kennedy and Johnson were elected.

President Kennedy gave Vice-President Johnson some important jobs to do. Johnson traveled to 27 countries on good-will trips.

President Kennedy was assassinated in Dallas in November 1963. Johnson was riding in a car behind Kennedy and was not injured. Lyndon Johnson took the oath of office aboard Air Force One, the presidential jet. He was the first president to be sworn in by a woman judge.

Johnson was often called by his initials, LBJ. He was a tall man with a big nose and large ears. He had a folksy way of speaking. Sometimes President Johnson walked around the White house turning off unneeded lights. He had two Beagles named Him and Her.

The Johnsons had two daughters, Lynda Bird and Luci. Both girls were married during their father's presidency. Luci had a huge White House wedding with 700 guests.

President Johnson was re-elected by a landslide in the 1964 election. He called his program the Great Society. He pushed civil rights laws through Congress. He created a program called the War on Poverty to help poor people. He helped improve schools and libraries with federal money. He also helped improve medical care for people over 65.

As First Lady, Lady Bird Johnson also worked to help the country. She started the Keep America Beautiful campaign. She worked on improvements for inner cities and for the preschool Head Start program.

During Johnson's years as president, the U.S. became more and more involved in the Vietnam War. Many people thought the war was wrong. Some blamed Johnson for the war. There were many anti-war demonstrations on college campuses. Some men refused to fight. The country had not been so divided since the Civil War.

President Johnson said he would not run for another term. He retired to the LBJ Ranch in Texas. On January 22, 1973, he died of a heart attack.

During Johnson's presidency (1963-1969)
-More than half a million U.S. soldiers were in Vietnam by 1968.
-North Korea seized the U.S. Navy ship *Pueblo*.

During 1963-1969:
-The Beatles made their first U.S. tour.
-Miniskirts were the latest fashion.
-The first *Spiderman* comic was printed.
-Dr. Martin Luther King, Jr. and Senator Robert F. Kennedy were assassinated.

RICHARD M. NIXON
(1969-1974)

37

Born: January 9, 1913
Party: Republican
Home state: California
Term of office: 1969-1974

"I never in my life wanted to be left behind."

Richard Nixon was born on a California fruit farm. He was one of five sons. His nickname was Dick.

The family moved to Whittier, California when Dick was nine. His father opened a gas station and a grocery store. Dick and his brothers helped in the store. They picked up vegetables early in the morning. They pumped gas after school.

Dick Nixon worked hard in school, too. His grades were excellent. He was a champion debater in high school and college. He also acted in plays.

At Whittier College, Nixon was elected president of the student body. He graduated second in his class. Then he went on to Duke University Law School in North Carolina. At Duke, he was known as "Gloomy Gus" because he always studied. He was third in his law school class when he graduated.

Nixon returned to Whittier and joined a law firm there. He also joined a theater group. There he met Pat Ryan, a high school teacher. Dick asked Pat to marry him the night they met. But it took two years before she said yes. In 1940 they were married. They had two daughters, Tricia and Julie. Tricia later had a White House wedding. Julie married David Eisenhower, the grandson of former President Eisenhower.

Nixon joined the Navy in World War II. He was in charge of building navy airstrips in the South Pacific. He advanced to the rank of lieutenant commander by the time the war ended.

Nixon entered politics by answering an ad in a newspaper. "Wanted: Congressional candidate with no previous experience." Nixon was the only person to respond. The Republican leaders agreed to sponsor him because he had a military record. He was elected to the House of Representatives in 1946.

In 1950 Nixon ran for the U.S. Senate. At thirty-seven he became the youngest Republican senator. In 1952 he was selected as Eisenhower's running mate. Nixon was Vice-President for eight years.

Nixon ran against Kennedy for president in 1960. Richard Nixon lost by the smallest margin ever in a presidential election. Two years later he ran for governor of California. He lost that election, too. Many people thought Nixon's career in politics was over. But in 1968 Nixon made a comeback. He was elected to the White House.

President Nixon faced some hard problems. There were many protests over the Vietnam War. The nation's rivers and lakes and air needed to be cleaned up. Inflation was rising. But the worst problem was yet to come.

Nixon was involved in the biggest presidential scandal ever. It started in 1972 during his successful run for re-election. The scandal was called Watergate.

The Democratic National Headquarters was located in the Watergate hotel-office building in Washington, D.C. In June 1972 five men broke into the headquarters and were arrested. They carried spy cameras and telephone tapping equipment. The burglars hoped to learn about the Democratic campaign.

Senate investigations later proved that members of Nixon's staff had ordered the break-in. The President knew they had ordered it. Nixon and his staff tried to cover up their part in Watergate. The Watergate burglars went to jail.

But the Watergate scandal was more than just the burglary and cover-up. There were other illegal or questionable acts in the Nixon White House. Illegal pay-offs had been made. Nixon and his staff had a list of political enemies they tried to embarrass. Vice-President Agnew resigned over charges of bribery and not paying income tax. Nixon himself had to pay almost half a million dollars in back income taxes. More "White House horrors" were discovered in congressional hearings and by the press. Many of Nixon's staff went to jail.

The Senate investigators discovered that Nixon had tapes of all conversations and phone calls that took place in his office. They wanted to listen to the tapes to learn more about who was involved in Watergate. The special Watergate prosecutor wanted to hear them, too. But Nixon refused to turn over the tapes. Finally the Supreme Court ruled that Nixon would have to obey the law and release the tapes.

In July 1974 the House of Representatives began impeachment proceedings against Nixon. Impeachment is the first step in removing a president from office. The House Judiciary Committee approved three articles of impeachment. But before the entire House could vote on impeachment, Nixon resigned his office. A month later President Ford granted Nixon a full presidential pardon. This meant that Nixon could not be taken to court or sent to jail for any of his illegal acts.

People will remember Nixon as the first president to resign from office. But his greatest success was in foreign policy. Nixon helped the U.S. become more friendly with the Soviet Union. He made a presidential visit to Moscow. Nixon also became the first president to visit the People's Republic of China. He helped Israel and Egypt stop fighting. And he helped to end the Vietnam War in 1973.

After leaving the White House, Nixon retired to his home in San Clemente, California. There he wrote a book about being president. In 1980 the Nixons moved to New York City to be closer to their daughters and grandchildren.

During Nixon's presidency (1969-1974)

- Apollo 11 astronauts took man's first walk on the moon.
- The United Nations recognized the People's Republic of China.
- President Nixon visited China and the Soviet Union.
- The Twenty-sixth Amendment to the U.S. Constitution was approved. It gave 18-year-olds the right to vote.

During 1969-1974:

- Patricia Hearst was kidnapped.
- Sixty-five airplanes were hijacked.
- Bobby Fischer became the first American world chess champion.

SECRET CODE

Use the code at the bottom of the page to find the message about a president. Each number stands for a letter.

$\overline{15}\ \overline{2}\ \overline{13}\ \overline{23}\ \overline{12}\ \overline{13}$ $\overline{17}\ \overline{12}\ \overline{19}\ \overline{13}\ \overline{8}\ \overline{12}\ \overline{13}$

$\overline{11}\ \overline{9}\ \overline{12}\ \overline{11}\ \overline{12}\ \overline{8}\ \overline{22}\ \overline{23}$

$\overline{14}\ \overline{26}\ \overline{9}\ \overline{9}\ \overline{18}\ \overline{26}\ \overline{20}\ \overline{22}$ $\overline{7}\ \overline{12}$

$\overline{15}\ \overline{26}\ \overline{23}\ \overline{2}$ $\overline{25}\ \overline{18}\ \overline{9}\ \overline{23}$ $\overline{12}\ \overline{13}$

$\overline{7}\ \overline{19}\ \overline{22}\ \overline{18}\ \overline{9}$ $\overline{21}\ \overline{18}\ \overline{9}\ \overline{8}\ \overline{7}$

$\overline{23}\ \overline{26}\ \overline{7}\ \overline{22}$.

26	25	24	23	22	21	20	19	18	17	16	15	14	13	12
A	B	C	D	E	F	G	H	I	J	K	L	M	N	O

11	10	9	8	7	6	5	4	3	2	1
P	Q	R	S	T	U	V	W	X	Y	Z

GERALD FORD
(1974-1977)

38

Born: July 14, 1913
Party: Republican
Home state: Michigan
Term of office: 1974-1977

"I'm the first Eagle Scout president of the U.S."

When this president was born, he was named Leslie
Lynch King, Jr. His parents were divorced when he was
two. Then his mother remarried and Leslie's stepfather
adopted him. He renamed the boy Gerald Rudolph
Ford, Jr. Ford was called Junior or "Junie" until he was
out of high school.

Ford was a handsome and popular young man. While
in high school he won a contest as the Most Popular
Senior and traveled to Washington to be honored.

During college, Ford and his girlfriend were photographed for an article in *Look* magazine.

Ford was a great athlete. He lettered in five sports in high school in Grand Rapids, Michigan. His best sport was football. He was a center for the state championship football team in high school. He went to the University of Michigan on a football scholarship. Ford was named Most Valuable Player in his senior year. He was offered contracts by the Green Bay Packers and the Detroit Lions. But he didn't play for either team. Instead he took a job as assistant football coach at Yale. He also coached freshman boxing.

While Ford was coaching at Yale he became interested in law. He asked if he could take a few law courses. He did so well, he was invited to study law in the college. Because he started late, he didn't graduate from law school until he was over 27.

In 1941 Ford set up a law practice in Grand Rapids, Michigan. But he closed it soon after World War II began. He enlisted in the Navy. His job was to get young recruits into shape for combat duty. He also served on an aircraft carrier in the Pacific.

After the war, Ford returned to practice law in Grand Rapids. The year 1948 was an important one for Jerry Ford. He married Betty Bloomer. He ran for office for the first time and was elected to the U.S. House of Representatives.

Ford's power in Congress grew over the years. In 1965, he became the minority leader of the House. He held that post until 1973. Then Gerald Ford replaced Spiro Agnew as Nixon's vice-president.

Ford was never elected to the presidency. He became

president when Richard Nixon resigned from office in 1974. Ford's role in history was to clean up the mess made by others. The Watergate scandal and the resignations of Agnew and Nixon had shattered people's faith. The economy was ready to plunge. Ford's job was to turn this situation around. He did the job in his two-year term.

President Ford brought a new openness and honesty to the White House. He wanted the American people to know what he did and why. He wanted to bring back faith in government. Ford had a personal touch that had been missing since the days of Kennedy and Johnson.

One of Ford's ideas was the WIN program. WIN meant Whip Inflation Now. This said that the average citizen, in little ways, could help beat inflation. Ford's idea was to involve everyone in working to fight the rising economic problems in this country. From all over the U.S. he received letters that proved people had listened.

Ford also pardoned Nixon. The pardon meant that Nixon could not be charged with any crimes committed during his presidency. Ford wanted Americans to look ahead and stop worrying about Nixon and Watergate.

The people liked to know about Jerry Ford and his family. Jerry and his four children loved to ski. Reporters always followed the Fords on their vacations in Vail, Colorado. Reporters were on hand when the President's golden retriever had puppies. And the reporters were also there for more serious problems in the Ford family.

When Betty Ford learned of her breast cancer, she told the American public. That sent thousands of women to their own doctors for examinations. Some found they had cancer, too. One of ... women was Vice-President Rockefeller's wife, ... Ford both had to have surgery. Do... She and ... told everyone about her illness ... glad by ov... Ford ... the risk of breast cancer. ... helped American public. ... ffered a nervous breakdown ... used Betty believed that it was b... to be honest with the American people. Gerald Ford tre...d the presidency in the same honest manner. That helped bring back faith in the government and the presidency.

Ford is over **six** feet tall and weighs 200 pounds. That is only four **pounds** over his football weight of forty years ago. He **loves** to ski and swims twice daily. He is a good golfer too. He admits that he doesn't like reading books but **loves** watching football on TV. Even as president he **always** read the sports section of the newspaper first.

Ford has unusual tastes in food. His favorite lunch is cottage cheese smothered in ketchup. He also likes to eat raw onions all by themselves. His favorite dessert is pecan ice cream with peach slices.

President Ford now lives in California and is an active Republican party member.

During Ford's presidency (1974-1977)
-Ford granted Nixon a presidential pardon for any Watergate crimes.
-Ford offered conditional amnesty to Vietnam War draft evaders.

During the Bear retired from public servi
movie *Star Wars* was released.
fish Hunter signed with the   York
nkees for 3.75 million de..nial.
The U.S. celebrated its

PRESIDENTIAL NICKNAMES

B. Harrison	Grandpa's Grandson
McKinley	Wobbly Willie
T. Roosevelt	Teddy
Wilson	Professor
Taft	Big Bill
Harding	President Hardly
Coolidge	Silent Cal
Hoover	Chief
F. Roosevelt	FDR
Truman	Give 'em Hell Harry
Eisenhower	Ike
Kennedy	JFK
L. Johnson	LBJ
Nixon	Tricky Dick
Ford	Eagle Scout President
Carter	Peanut President
Reagan	Movie Star President

WORD SEARCH

Find the presidents and their First Ladies hidden below.

```
R   E   W   O   H   N   E   S   I   E
K   G   E   R   A   L   D   J   B   D
E   F   Y   T   T   E   B   J   P   D
N   J   O   H   N   S   O   N   R   B
N   D   D   R   A   H   C   I   R   N
E   N   I   X   O   N   B   P   A   T
D   H   E   Z   J   Y   D   R   O   F
Y   O   K   D   D   M   A   M   I   E
F   J   I   A   J   A   C   K   I   E
Y   J   L   Y   N   D   O   N   S   W
```

Ford	Betty	Gerald
Johnson	Lady Bird	Lyndon
Nixon	Pat	Richard
Kennedy	Jackie	John
Eisenhower	Mamie	Ike

JIMMY CARTER
(1977-1981)

39

Born: October 1, 1924
Party: Democratic
Home state: Georgia
Term of office: 1977-1981

"I will never lie to the American people."

Jimmy Carter was born on October 1, 1924. He was the first president born in a hospital instead of at home. His full name is James Earl Carter, Jr., but he prefers just Jimmy Carter.

His family was poor when he was young. Their house had no electricity or running water. The Carters were peanut farmers. They also owned a small grocery store in town. Everyone worked to help support the family.

Jimmy started learning about business at a young

age. When he was six, he started selling peanuts at a nickel a bag on the streets of Plains, Georgia. By the time he was nine he had saved enough money to buy five bales of cotton. He sold the cotton a few years later after the price tripled.

Carter attended Plains High School. The school's principal, Julia Coleman, had a big influence on Jimmy. She made him listen to classical music. She made sure he knew the names of all the best artists, musicians, and composers. She also gave Carter many books to read. One was *War and Peace*. It is still his favorite book.

From the time he was five, Carter wanted to be an officer in the Navy. When he was six, he wrote to the U.S. Naval Academy at Annapolis. He asked for an application. The academy wrote back that he should apply when he graduated from high school. He entered the Naval Academy in 1943.

During one Christmas vacation Jimmy started dating his sister's best friend, Rosalynn Smith. They were married a month after Jimmy's graduation from the Naval Academy.

Carter served in the Navy for the next seven years. He worked as an electronics instructor and as an engineering officer aboard atomic-powered submarines. Rosalynn and Jimmy had three sons during their navy years. Later they had a daughter, Amy. Both parents consider the night of Amy's birth the happiest in their lives.

In 1953 Carter's father died. Carter resigned his commission in the Navy. He returned to Plains to run the family business. He and Rosalynn worked hard together. They bought peanuts from other farmers in the area and sold them to processors. Rosalynn took care of all the business records. She has continued to help her husband throughout his career.

In 1962 Carter entered politics. He was elected that year to the Georgia State Senate. He served two terms. His involvement in politics grew. In 1966 he ran against Lester Maddox for the Democratic nomination for governor. He lost. In 1970 he tried again. This time he succeeded. He went on to win the general election.

Carter spent four years as governor. He had new ideas for Georgia. He reorganized the state government. Industry grew. Farmers made more money. The people of Georgia liked Carter and his ideas. Carter thought his ideas would work for the whole country.

Carter began his campaign for president in 1974. But not many people outside Georgia knew who he was. He was not from Washington. He had never received much publicity as governor. But people liked him. He could talk to people who were different from himself. He could get ideas across to them. And he had strong beliefs. He wanted to cut taxes. He wanted to help minority groups. He said that government should serve the people better.

Carter beat Gerald Ford in the 1976 presidential election. The vote was close. Carter won the election by a hundred thousand votes. Only two years before, people had asked, "Jimmy who?" Now he was their president.

Carter had successful and unsuccessful times as president. His biggest success was in foreign affairs. He helped Egypt and Israel reach an historic peace agreement.

But things in the U.S. got worse. Inflation grew. Big corporations had to lay off workers. Carter could not solve the country's economic problems.

Carter's biggest problem was in the Middle Eastern country of Iran. On November 4, 1979, the American Embassy in Iran was taken over by armed students. The Iranians held 52 Americans hostage for over 14 months. In the last hours of Carter's presidency, the United States and Iran reached an agreement for the release of the hostages.

In 1980 Carter ran for president again. He ran against Ronald Reagan. All the polls said the election would be close. But the polls were wrong. Carter was defeated in a Reagan landslide. Republicans won congressional seats all over the country. The Democrats lost control of the Senate for the first time in 25 years. The country was ready for a change.

During Carter's presidency (1977-1981)
- Israel and Egypt reached a peace agreement at Camp David.
- The U.S. boycotted the Summer Olympics in Moscow because of the Soviet occupation of Afghanistan.
- The American Embassy in Iran was taken over by the Iranians. Embassy workers were held hostage for over 14 months.

During 1977-1981:
- Voyager I took the first close-up pictures of Uranus and Saturn.
- Elvis Presley and John Lennon died.
- The U.S. hockey team won a gold medal in the Winter Olympics.
- Mt. St. Helens became an active volcano.

RONALD REAGAN
(1981-   )

40

Born: February 6, 1911
Party: Republican
Home state: California
Term of office: 1981-

"I'm not smart enough to lie."

Ronald Reagan was born February 6, 1911 in Tampico, Illinois. He and his older brother, Neil, loved playing in the woods near Tampico and fishing in a nearby creek.

When Ronald was nine, his family moved to a larger town named Dixon. At Dixon High School Reagan played football and basketball and went out for track and swimming.

At 14 Ronald got his first job, digging foundations for new houses. The summer he was 15, Reagan found a job as a lifeguard. He kept that job for seven summers, and he saved 77 people from drowning.

Ronald saved the money he earned. He wanted to go to Eureka College in Illinois. He started college there in 1928. He worked his way through school as a dishwasher, lifeguard, and swimming coach. Reagan was a star player on the football team. And he also acted in plays.

His first job after graduation was announcing football games for a small radio station in Davenport, Iowa. Soon he was hired as a full-time staff announcer. Later he worked for a bigger station in Des Moines.

On a visit to Hollywood, Reagan met an agent and had a screen test. He was offered a movie contract and moved to California. His first movie was called *Love Is On the Air*. He made eight movies in 11 months. Reagan played a radio announcer in *Hollywood Hotel* and a military school cadet in a comedy called *Brother Rat.*

One of the actresses from this film was Jane Wyman. She and Reagan were married. They had a daughter, Maureen, in 1941 and adopted a son, Michael, in 1945. Their marriage ended in divorce.

Reagan made over 50 films during his career. He often played cowboys or soldiers. One of his famous movies was called *Bedtime for Bonzo.* Bonzo was a chimpanzee and he became a star, too.

During World War II Reagan helped make training films for the Air Force. Later he worked in television. He starred in a series called *Death Valley Days.* He was also the host for *General Electric Theater.*

Reagan was active in the Screen Actors Guild, a union for movie actors. He worked on getting better benefits for actors and actresses. He also made many speeches all over the country.

In 1952 Reagan married an actress named Nancy Davis. They have two children: Patti, who is an actress and Ron, who is a ballet dancer.

Reagan began his political career in 1966. He was elected governor of California. He won the election by over one million votes. As governor, he cut taxes. He also reduced welfare costs. He became very popular as governor and easily won a second term in 1970.

In 1976 Reagan tried for the Republican nomination for president. The nomination went to Gerald Ford, who was then president. In 1980 Reagan tried again. This time the Republicans nominated him. He won in a landslide victory over President Carter.

Reagan stands for changes in the United States. He wants less government control of business and industry. He wants more national defense spending. He also wants a big tax cut for the American people.

Ronald Reagan is the first movie actor to become president. Reagan is the first divorced man to become president. He is also the oldest president to be elected to office. President Reagan was two weeks away from his 70th birthday when he took the oath of office.

PRESIDENTIAL FACTS

1. He was the smallest president.

_____

2. He was the tallest president.

_____

3. He was the fattest president.

_____

4. He was the handsomest president.

_____

5. He lived longer than any other president.

_____

6. He died at a younger age than any other president.

_____

7. He was in office for the shortest term.

_____

8. He was in office for the longest term.

_____

ANSWERS

Presidential Money Match, page 13:
Lincoln, Jefferson, F.D. Roosevelt, Washington, Washington, Jefferson, Lincoln, Jackson

Word Scramble, page 24:
Madison, Washington, John Adams, Monroe, Jefferson, Dolley, Martha, Mt. Vernon, Abigail, First Lady, President, Monticello, White House, Independence, Flag

Name Game, page 28:
a, ad, am, an, and, as, dam, dams, dim, dims, din, I, in, is, mad, maid, maids, man, mason, no, nod, nods, on, sad, sin, so, sod, son

Word Find, page 33:

Presidential Top Ten, page 41:
1. Washington, 2. J. Adams, 3. Jefferson, 4. Madison, 5. Monroe, 6. J.Q. Adams, 7. Jackson, 8. Van Buren, 9. W.H. Harrison, 10. Tyler

Trivia Brain Buster, page 44:
1. Jackson, 2. Madison, 3. Polk

Quick Quiz, page 47:
1. James Madison, 2. John Quincy Adams

Morse Code Puzzle, page 54:
George Washington was the Father of Our Country.

Presidential Quiz, page 67:
1. Andrew Johnson, 2. Lincoln, 3. Van Buren, 4. Polk, 5. Madison, 6. William Henry Harrison, 7. Washington, 8. Tyler, 9. Fillmore, 10. Pierce, 11. John Quincy Adams

True or False, page 77:
1. True, 2. False, 3. True

Presidential Name Game, page 95:
Van Buren, Polk, Grant, Cleveland, Hayes, Lincoln, Buchanan, McKinley, Arthur, Jackson, Tyler, Garfield, Pierce, Fillmore, Taylor

Match Game, page 102:
Abraham Lincoln, James Polk, Theodore Roosevelt, Zachary Taylor, Franklin Pierce, Ulysses Grant, John Tyler, Grover Cleveland, Thomas Jefferson, Millard Fillmore, Martin Van Buren, Woodrow Wilson, Rutherford Hayes, Chester Arthur, Andrew Jackson

Trivia Time, page 105:
Washington, Jefferson, Lincoln, and Theodore Roosevelt.

Fourth of July Facts, page 109:
1. Calvin Coolidge (July 4, 1872); 2. John Adams (July 4, 1826), Thomas Jefferson (July 4, 1826), James Monroe (July 4, 1831); 3. Ulysses S. Grant

Home States, page 119:
New York—Van Buren, Fillmore, Arthur, Cleveland, T. Roosevelt, F. Roosevelt
Virginia—Washington, Jefferson, Madison, Monroe, Tyler
Ohio—W. Harrison, Hayes, Garfield, McKinley, Taft, Harding

College Quiz, page 133:

1. Thomas Jefferson (The University of Virginia)
2. Harvard University (J. Adams, J.Q. Adams, T. Roosevelt, F.D. Roosevelt, J.F. Kennedy)
3. Jefferson (University of Virginia), Garfield (Hiram College), Wilson (Princeton University), and Eisenhower (Columbia University)
4. Washington, Jackson, Van Buren, Taylor, Fillmore, Lincoln, Andrew Johnson, Cleveland, Truman

Secret Code, page 143:

Lyndon Johnson proposed marriage to Lady Bird on their first date.

Word Search, page 149:

```
R E W O H N E S I E
K G E R A L D J B D
E F Y T T E B J P D
N J O H N S O N R B
N D D R A H C I R N
E N I X O N B P A T
D H E Z J Y D R O F
Y O K D D M A M I E
F J I A J A C K I E
Y J L Y N D O N S W
```

Presidential Facts, page 157:

1. Madison (5'4" under 100 lbs), 2. Lincoln (6'4"), 3. Taft (over 325 lbs), 4. Kennedy (a matter of opinion), 5. John Adams (age 91), 6. Kennedy (age 46), 7. W. Harrison (March-April 1841), 8. F. Roosevelt (elected to 4 terms)